BUILD:
YOUR EMPIRE

GROW:
YOUR BRAND

MAXIMIZE:
YOUR RESULTS

Table of Contents

Chapter ONE: Introduction........................... 1

Chapter TWO: The Foundation of Profitability – The Impact Beyond the Numbers................. 11

Chapter THREE: Pillar 1: Mindset - Shifting Perspectives: From Scarcity to Abundance ... 26

Chapter FOUR: Pillar 2: Marketing Systems - Marketing Systems - The Blueprint for Visibility ….. 46

Chapter FIVE: Pillar 3: Sales Systems - Constructing the Deal............................ 72

Chapter SIX: Pillar 4: Knowing Your Numbers - The Financial Framework….................... 110

Chapter SEVEN: Pillar 5: Your Team - The Builders of Your Vision…...................... 135

Chapter EIGHT: Bring It All Together With Consistency…………………….............. 151

Chapter NINE: The Power of Action and Implementation ………………....…...... 156

In Conclusion 160

Foundation First: The 5 Pillars of Unstoppable Growth in Your Home Improvement Business

Welcome to "Foundation First: The 5 Pillars of Unstoppable Growth in Your Home Improvement Business."

An empowering and comprehensive guide crafted specifically for dedicated professionals like you—painters, roofers, kitchen remodelers, bathroom remodelers, flooring installers, and other experts in the home improvement industry.

As you embark on the often-challenging journey of entrepreneurship, this book is designed to be your indispensable roadmap, steering you not just towards survival, but towards achieving unparalleled success and long-term profitability in your field.

Imagine running a business where every ounce of effort translates into substantial financial rewards, where each completed project not only enhances your clients' living spaces but also drives your company to new heights of success.

This vision is entirely within your grasp, and it all begins with adopting the five essential pillars: mindset, marketing systems, sales systems, knowing your numbers, and cultivating your team.

Ultimately, unstoppable growth is about envisioning the future and taking proactive steps to shape it. It's about being resilient in the face of setbacks and maintaining a clear vision of your goals.

With the principles outlined in "Foundation First," you'll be equipped to harness the full potential of your business, driving it towards a future filled with limitless possibilities and continuous achievements.

With these tools, you'll be empowered to not only establish a strong brand but also elevate your business to unprecedented levels of success while elevating your role as a leader.

So, ask yourself—Are you ready to invest in your growth, grasp the fundamentals, and continually strive for improvement?

If there's any doubt, let "Foundation First" be your guiding light, illuminating the path to unlocking your business's full potential and ensuring a prosperous future.

Chapter ONE: Introduction

In 2009, I began the thrilling yet challenging venture of launching a home improvement business.

Driven by determination and the notion that success was a solo pursuit, I immersed myself in the demanding routine of running a one-person operation, handling every aspect of the business. I believed this method epitomized true entrepreneurial spirit.

However, as time went by, I encountered numerous obstacles and faced slow progress. It was during these trying times that I grasped a vital truth: sustainable growth doesn't stem from going it alone but from investing in oneself and learning from others.

The hardship of those early years cannot be overstated. Consistently generating leads was a constant struggle, and the uncertainty of income left me living check to check.

The financial instability took its toll, forcing me to work nights and weekends to make ends meet. This relentless schedule meant missing precious family moments, and the isolation of managing everything on my own began to weigh heavily on me.

The dream of entrepreneurship was overshadowed by the harsh reality of burnout and the creeping doubt that perhaps I had bitten off more than I could chew.

A pivotal moment in my journey arrived when I chose to break free from my self-imposed isolation. I dived into books, participated in industry events, and sought mentorship. This period was truly eye-opening, unveiling a wealth of knowledge and resources at my disposal.

Investing in myself, both financially and emotionally, turned the tide. The years spent grappling in solitude paled in comparison to the remarkable progress I made through education and collaboration.

This shift in mindset was revolutionary, leading not only to business success but also to a significant personal transformation. The newfound balance allowed me to reclaim family time and build a more sustainable and fulfilling business.

Motivated by my experiences and the profound impact of personal growth investment, I felt a strong desire to empower other home improvement contractors.

Understanding the challenges they encountered—loneliness and uncertainty—I shared my insights, determined to make a difference.

By emphasizing mindset, systems, and strategies, my goal is to illuminate the path for others, demonstrating that with the right approach, anyone can develop, expand, and maximize their life, business, and potential.

This mission transcended mere career aspirations; it became a calling to inspire change and cultivate a community where success is a collective voyage, not a solitary struggle.

Reflecting on my journey, I am immensely proud of how far I have come and the lessons I have learned along the way.

The transition from struggling in isolation to thriving through collaboration has been transformative not only for my business but also for my personal growth.

This profound shift inspired me to write "Foundation First: The 5 Pillars of Building a Profitable Home Improvement Business".

This book is designed to be a guiding light for home improvement business owners, illuminating the path to sustainable and profitable growth.

"Foundation First" is born out of my desire to help entrepreneurs maximize their business potential while minimizing the time and struggles associated with going it alone.

The five pillars I discuss are the foundation of a thriving business: mindset, systems, strategies, community, and continuous learning.

By embracing these principles, I believe that any home improvement business owner can achieve remarkable success and reclaim their personal life, just as I did.

Ultimately, my mission is to empower others with the knowledge and resources to build a business that not only sustains them financially but also enriches their lives.

I want to foster a supportive and collaborative environment where business owners can learn from each other, grow together, and celebrate their successes.

My hope is that "Foundation First" will serve as a valuable tool in this journey, helping entrepreneurs transform their dreams into reality and create a legacy of success for future generations.

Laying the Foundation: The Five Pillars Approach

Creating a profitable business is much like constructing a sturdy home; it starts with a strong foundation. Each layer added must be meticulously planned and executed.

Just as a home requires sturdy materials and skilled craftsmanship to be constructed, a business needs unified team members, innovative products or services, and efficient processes to grow and thrive.

It's essential to monitor progress, adapt to changes, and continuously improve to maintain strength and stability.

Cultivating strong relationships with clients, suppliers, and stakeholders acts as the reinforcing beams that support the structure. Transparency, trust, and exceptional service lay the groundwork for lasting partnerships and a loyal customer base.

As your business scales, the challenges may become more complex, much like the increasing difficulty in constructing higher levels of a home.

However, with a resilient foundation, strategic planning, and a commitment to excellence, a business can ascend to great heights, achieving both profitability and sustainability.

In this section you will learn how these foundational elements interlock to support and elevate your contracting business, guiding you toward profitability and the achievement of your goals.

Pillar 1: Mindset - The Architect of Your Reality

The journey to profitability starts within. A contractor's mindset is the foundation of their success. Cultivating a growth mindset empowers you to view challenges as opportunities, fostering resilience and adaptability. Embracing continuous learning and staying open to innovation propels your business forward. This mental fortitude prepares you to effectively leverage the subsequent pillars, ensuring that your business is not just surviving, but thriving.

Pillar 2: Marketing Systems - The Blueprint for Visibility

In the digital age, a well-structured marketing system acts as your business's blueprint for visibility and engagement. Effective marketing strategies encompass a thorough understanding of your target market, compelling branding, and the seamless integration of digital and traditional marketing techniques. By consistently refining your marketing approach, you attract quality leads, creating a steady pipeline that fuels your business's growth.

Pillar 3: Sales Systems - Constructing the Deal

With a robust marketing system attracting leads, your sales system is where potential projects are converted into contracts. A streamlined sales process, characterized by clear communication and an understanding of client needs, builds trust and facilitates the closing of deals. Training your team in effective sales techniques ensures that your business can consistently secure profitable projects, laying the groundwork for long-term success.

Pillar 4: Knowing Your Numbers - The Financial Framework

A profitable contracting business has its finger on the pulse of its financial health. Understanding your numbers—costs, margins, cash flow, and projections—provides the clarity needed to make informed decisions. Implementing financial systems for regular monitoring and analysis ensures you can adjust strategies promptly, optimize profitability, and avoid potential pitfalls. This financial acumen acts as the framework supporting the sustainability and growth of your enterprise.

Pillar 5: Your Team - The Builders of Your Vision

The final pillar, Your Team, emphasizes the importance of cultivating a skilled, motivated, and cohesive workforce. Your team is the lifeblood of your business, turning vision into reality. Investing in their development, fostering a positive culture, and aligning their goals with those of the business amplifies productivity and innovation. Recognizing and rewarding their contributions builds loyalty and dedication, propelling your business towards its objectives.

The Blueprint for Success

The combination of these five pillars creates a sturdy foundation for any contracting business.

Each pillar depends on the others, forming a comprehensive approach that promotes growth, profitability, and resilience.

By committing to the continuous improvement in these areas, you not only set the stage for immediate success but also secure the longevity and sustainability of your business.

Embrace this five-pillar approach, and watch as your contracting business transforms from a vision into a profitable reality.

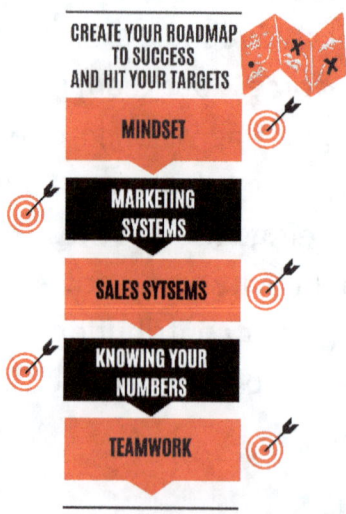

Chapter TWO: The Foundation of Profitability – The Impact Beyond the Numbers

Understanding the importance of building a profitable business is critical. A profitable business is not just a measure of success; it's the catalyst for sustainable growth, financial stability, and the achievement of long-term goals.

This discussion explores why profitability is crucial for your home improvement business and the unlimited benefits it can bring to both your professional and personal life.

First and foremost, profitability ensures the financial health of your business. It provides the essential capital needed for reinvestment, enabling you to purchase advanced tools, adopt new technologies, and hire skilled labor.

These investments are vital for staying competitive in the ever-evolving home improvement market. Healthy profit margins act as a safety net during economic downturns or when unexpected expenses arise, ensuring your business can weather tough times.

A profitable business brings peace of mind to both owners and employees. It fosters a stable work environment where employees feel secure, leading to higher morale, increased productivity, and reduced turnover.

For you, the business owner, profitability translates into personal financial security, enabling you to provide for your family, plan for the future, and enjoy a comfortable lifestyle.

This security allows you to focus on strategic planning, business development, and personal goals without the constant worry of financial instability.

Ultimately, profitability is the key to achieving long-term business and personal aspirations.

Whether your goals are to expand your business, enter new markets, or engage in philanthropic activities, a profitable business generates the necessary resources to pursue these endeavors.

It also establishes your business as a reputable and reliable entity in the industry, attracting potential clients and partners

In essence, profitability is about more than just numbers; it's about building a legacy, making a difference, and realizing your dreams.

As you dive into the strategies for building a profitable home improvement business, remember that each strategy, decision, and action should ultimately contribute to this fundamental objective.

The Far-reaching Benefits of Profitability

When you build a successful business, you create a ripple effect that extends far beyond your own personal gains.

The results of your hard work will significantly and enduringly impact not only your own life but also the lives of your family, your team, and your clients.

Let's explore the diverse and significant advantages of building a successful and profitable business, and how doing so can positively impact a wide range of people and communities.

For You: A Foundation of Financial Freedom

As the owner of a home improvement business, you are the most immediate beneficiary of profitability. This financial stability provides a solid foundation upon which you can build your dreams.

It's not just about living a life of luxury; it's about gaining the financial freedom to make choices that align with your values and aspirations.

Whether it's investing in advanced training, exploring new markets, or simply having the peace of mind that comes with financial security, profitability opens up a world of possibilities.

It allows you to take calculated risks, innovate, and steer your business in exciting new directions without the crippling fear of financial ruin.

For Your Family: The Ripple Effect of Success

The impact your family will receive from having a profitable home improvement business are profound and far-reaching.

Financial stability extends beyond simply covering daily necessities; it encompasses the ability to secure your family's future, from funding education and healthcare to creating cherished memories together.

Profitability transforms your lifestyle from merely surviving to truly thriving. It allows you to work less and spend more quality time with your loved ones, strengthening relationships and building a legacy.

Additionally, your success serves as a powerful example to your children, teaching them the value of hard work, perseverance, and the rewards of entrepreneurship.

For Your Team: Cultivating a Culture of Growth and Opportunity

A profitable business is a huge benefit to your team. Offering job security, competitive salaries, and opportunities for professional growth.

Profitability allows you to invest in their development, equipping them with the skills and knowledge to excel in their roles and advance their careers. This not only enhances their personal and professional lives but also fosters loyalty, productivity, and innovation within your organization.

A thriving business can afford to reward its team, creating a positive, motivating work environment where everyone feels valued and invested in the company's success.

For Your Clients: Delivering Excellence and Value

The benefits of your profitability extend to your clients as well. A financially stable business can focus on quality, innovation, and customer service, rather than cutting corners to stay afloat.

This commitment to excellence elevates the standard of your work, setting you apart in a competitive market. Happy, satisfied clients are more likely to return and refer others, fueling further growth and profitability.

A successful business can afford to give back to the community, whether through charitable initiatives or pro bono work, enhancing your reputation and making a positive impact beyond your bottom line.

The pursuit of profitability in your home improvement business is a noble endeavor with wide-reaching benefits.

It's about much more than personal gain; it's about creating a positive ripple effect that touches the lives of your family, your team, your clients, and your community.

By focusing on the foundational pillars of building a profitable business, you set the stage for a legacy of success, impact, and fulfillment.

Mastering the 50% Gross Profit Margin

Mastering the art of strategic pricing is essential for any thriving business. In this section, we explore the pivotal practice of setting your project prices to secure a 50% gross margin.

This strategy can profoundly enhance your company's financial stability and long-term success. By adopting this approach, you'll be well on your way to ensuring sustained profitability and growth.

A 50% gross margin means that for every dollar of revenue your project generates, fifty cents are gross profit, before accounting for the indirect costs and expenses of running your business.

To sell at a 50% gross margin, you first need to have a clear understanding of your direct costs—materials, labor, and subcontractors. Once these costs are accurately calculated, pricing your services to achieve the 50% margin involves setting your selling price at double the direct cost.

For instance, if the direct cost of a project is $10,000, your selling price should be $20,000 to achieve a 50% gross margin.

Adopting a 50% gross margin strategy carries a plethora of benefits crucial for the growth and stability of your contracting business. It ensures that your business has a healthy cash flow, which is the oxygen of any enterprise.

This margin allows for the coverage of overhead costs, such as office expenses, insurance, and salaries, while also ensuring that there's enough left for reinvestment into the business for growth and innovation.

A 50% margin provides a safety net that can help your business weather economic downturns and unexpected expenses, which are inevitable in the contracting industry.

However, selling at a 50% gross margin is not just about setting the right price; it's also about value perception. Your clients need to perceive the value of your services as worth the cost.

This requires excellent communication of the quality, reliability, and distinctiveness of your services.

It's about building trust and demonstrating that choosing your business is not merely an expense but an investment in quality and peace of mind.

To support this perception, invest in skilled labor, high-quality materials, and a customer-centric approach to project management.

Pricing your projects to achieve a 50% gross margin is a foundational strategy for building a profitable contracting business.

It ensures financial health, provides a buffer against uncertainties, and supports business growth and development.

By understanding your costs, setting the right prices, and communicating the value of your services, you can establish a strong and profitable business that stands the test of time.

Remember, the goal is not just to survive in the competitive contracting industry but to thrive and set new benchmarks of success.

Two Tales of Construction

Every entrepreneur dreams of building a business that not only survives but thrives.

Within this section, we weave together two contrasting narratives: the story of John, a contractor who grapples with the challenges of profitability, and the tale of Sarah, a visionary contractor who harnesses the power of the 5 Pillars to construct a flourishing enterprise.

John's journey begins with passion and promise. Armed with technical expertise and a vision for his business, he dives into the world of contracting.

However, as time progresses, John finds himself ensnared in a cycle of missed opportunities and financial strain.

His approach, though well-intentioned, lacks structure—his mindset is fixed, his marketing sporadic, sales strategies undefined, financial understanding superficial, and his team feels directionless.

John's story serves as a touching reminder of the challenging journey many contractors endure, as they strive to establish themselves in a highly competitive market.

In contrast, Sarah's story is one of purposeful action and strategic growth. From the outset, she embraces a growth mindset, viewing challenges as opportunities to evolve.

Sarah knows the importance of a solid foundation; she dedicates time to building effective marketing systems that consistently attract leads, sets up sales processes that turn prospects into devoted customers, carefully tracks her financial status to make well-informed decisions, and fosters a team environment centered on collaboration and a common vision.

Her business doesn't merely expand—it flourishes, serving as a shining example of the transformative impact of the 5 Pillars.

When we compare these narratives, an important question arises: Which story sounds familiar, and more importantly, which story would you like yours to resemble?

John's tale is a cautionary reminder of the pitfalls that await when foundational elements are overlooked. Sarah's success, conversely, underscores the profound impact of building your business on the 5 Pillars.

The journey from struggle to success is not merely a change in tactics but a holistic transformation in how a contracting business is conceived, built, and grown.

Challenges and Change: Embracing a Structured Approach

In reflecting on John's and Sarah's contrasting journeys, I found myself deeply resonating with their stories.

As an entrepreneur, I have experienced both the highs and lows of building a business.

Much like John, there were times when I felt overwhelmed by all challenges that came my way. My initial enthusiasm was often dampened by missed opportunities and financial struggles.

I lacked the structured approach necessary to navigate the complexities of running a business, and my team, though talented, lacked a unified direction.

The turning point in my entrepreneurial journey came when I decided to embrace the principles exemplified by Sarah.

This transformation was not instantaneous, nor was it without its challenges. However, with persistence and a clear strategic framework, my business began to thrive.

We saw a steady increase in profitability, a more cohesive team dynamic, and a brand reputation that attracted new clients.

As I look back, I realize that the journey to success is as much about personal growth and mindset as it is about business acumen.

By building on a solid foundation and adhering to the 5 Pillars, any entrepreneur can turn their vision into a thriving reality.

Whether you see yourself in John, Sarah, or somewhere in between, the path to a profitable and sustainable contracting business begins with a choice to build on a solid "Foundation First."

In the chapters that follow, we'll dive deeper into each of the 5 Pillars, equipping you with the knowledge, strategies, and tools to write your own story of success.

Chapter THREE: Pillar 1: Mindset - Shifting Perspectives: From Scarcity to Abundance

In your journey to build a profitable contracting business, the foundation of all endeavors rests not just in the physical tools and resources at your disposal, but, most crucially, in the power of your mindset.

This pivotal chapter of "Foundation First," is dedicated to the business owners who are ready to lay the foundation of their success with the strength of their thoughts, beliefs, and attitudes.

We dive deep into the essence of cultivating a mindset inspired by positivity, abundance, proactivity, and an unwavering commitment to growth.

As you navigate the complexities of developing and expanding your contracting business, you will face challenges that test your resolve, often tempting you to fall into negativity or a scarcity mindset.

It is precisely in these moments that the principles discussed in this chapter will serve as your guiding light.

With engaging insights and practical strategies, this chapter seeks to transform your perspective, enabling you to face each obstacle with confidence and seize every opportunity with enthusiasm.

The transition from a fixed mindset, which perceives obstacles as insurmountable, to a growth mindset, which views challenges as opportunities for growth, is both transformative and enriching.

This chapter is not just about theoretical concepts; it serves a practical guide designed to inspire you to take action.

By embracing a positive, abundant, proactive, and growth-oriented mindset, you unlock the potential to not only achieve your business goals but to surpass them.

Remember, the foundation of a thriving contracting business is not laid with bricks and mortar alone but is fortified by the strength, resilience, and expansiveness of the owner's mindset.

Let this guide you in nurturing the mindset that will become the foundation of your business's success.

Embracing the Shift: From Employee to Entrepreneurial Mindset

Understanding the difference between an entrepreneurial mindset and an employee mindset is crucial for success.

The heart of an entrepreneurial mindset lies in seeing the bigger picture, embracing risks, and driving innovation.

In contrast, the employee mindset is often characterized by a quest for stability, adherence to defined roles, and a focus on task execution.

This fundamental difference in perspective can markedly influence the trajectory of your business growth.

Embracing an entrepreneurial mindset catapults business owners into a realm where every challenge transforms into an opportunity for growth.

Shifting from a safety-first, task-oriented employee mindset to a boundary-pushing, opportunity-seeking entrepreneurial mindset can significantly accelerate business development.

It nurtures a culture of ongoing learning, adaptability, and resilience. These key traits are needed in today's rapidly changing business landscape.

Embracing an entrepreneurial mindset promotes visionary leadership that motivates teams, draws in creative talent, and builds a competitive advantage, driving a business to achieve unprecedented success.

To help you in this transformative shift, here are two steps business owners can undertake:

1. **Cultivate a Visionary Outlook:**
   Begin by defining a clear, compelling vision for your business that goes beyond mere profitability. Consider the impact you want to make in your industry or community. This vision will serve as your north star, guiding your decisions and inspiring innovation. Encourage your team to think in terms of possibilities rather than limitations. This can be achieved through regular brainstorming sessions where no idea is too bold, and creativity is rewarded.
2. **Embrace Risks and Learn from Failure:**
   Shifting to an entrepreneurial mindset requires a fundamental reevaluation of risk and failure. Instead of perceiving them as setbacks, view them as essential stepping stones to success. Foster an environment where taking calculated risks is encouraged, and failures are analyzed for learning opportunities rather than penalized. This approach not only drives innovation but also builds resilience within the team, preparing your business to navigate through uncertainties more effectively.

Shifting from thinking like an employee to adopting an entrepreneurial mindset goes beyond just changing how you think; it's a strategic step to fully realize your business's potential.

This transformation demands a conscious effort to develop a forward-thinking perspective and foster an environment that takes risks and learns from mistakes. Embracing this new mindset can pave the way for significant growth, innovation, and enduring success, establishing a strong foundation for a prosperous approach.

Cultivating a Growth Mindset for Contracting Success

The path of a contracting business is filled with obstacles, uncertainties, and intense competition. Dury this challenging journey, one critical factor that differentiates the successful from the rest is the mindset of the business owner.

This section explores the transformative impact of a growth mindset in building a thriving contracting business.

At the heart of a growth mindset lies the belief that abilities and intelligence can be developed through dedication, hard work, and perseverance.

This perspective embraces challenges, persists despite setbacks, learns from criticism, and draws lessons and inspiration from the success of others.

Embracing a growth mindset starts with valuing persistence over innate talent.

In the early stages of building your business, you will inevitably face obstacles that seem insurmountable.

Whether it's securing your first major contract, navigating regulatory challenges, or managing workforce issues, persistence is key.

With a growth mindset, setbacks become opportunities for learning and growth rather than insurmountable barriers.

This approach nurtures a culture of innovation within your organization, encouraging your team to seek out new solutions and approaches instead of being discouraged by failure.

A growth mindset empowers you to view change and uncertainty as natural parts of business growth.

Seeing these changes as opportunities rather than threats can make the difference between stagnation and growth.

It encourages continuous learning for yourself and your team, ensuring that your business stays competitive and at the forefront of industry advancements.

Adopting a growth mindset is not just a personal development goal; it is a strategic necessity for contracting business owners.

It lays the foundation for a resilient, adaptable, and innovative business capable of overcoming challenges and seizing opportunities.

As you continue to build and expand your contracting business, let the principles of a growth mindset guide your decisions, shape your leadership, and inspire your team.

Remember, success in the contracting industry is not just about the contracts you secure but about the mindset with which you pursue them.

Cultivating an Abundant Mindset for Growth

The key to distinguishing between stagnation and growth often lies within your mind. Embracing an abundant mindset is not merely advantageous; it is critical for the expansion and success of your business.

This section explores the transformative potential of an abundant mindset and offers practical strategies for integrating this perspective into your daily operations.

An abundant mindset is rooted in the belief that there is ample success, resources, and opportunities available for everyone.

This sharply contrasts with a scarcity mindset, which perceives success as a limited commodity.

While a scarcity mindset limits possibilities and fosters competition, an abundant mindset paves the way for collaboration, innovation, and, ultimately, growth.

By embracing the notion of abundance, you can look beyond immediate obstacles and focus on long-term growth strategies.

To develop an abundant mindset, begin by recognizing your current achievements and strengths. Acknowledging what you have accomplished thus far provides a strong foundation for future growth.

It is also important to surround yourself with individuals who share this positive outlook, as their perspectives can influence your thinking and help maintain your focus on abundance.

Additionally, practicing gratitude regularly helps you appreciate what you have and the opportunities around you, conditioning your mind to notice and attract more positive outcomes.

Adopting an abundant mindset means being open to learning and adapting. Those who view changes and challenges as opportunities to grow will thrive.

This involves being willing to invest in your own development and that of your team, exploring new markets, and being innovative in your approach to business.

Embracing risk as a part of growth and viewing failures as lessons rather than setbacks are also key aspects of an abundant mindset.

Cultivating an abundant mindset is a powerful strategy for growing your contracting business. It enables you to transcend limitations, seize opportunities, and build a thriving, resilient empire.

Remember, abundance is not just about having more; it's about being more. By fostering an environment of growth, learning, and positivity, you lay down the foundation for a successful and expansive future.

Start today, and watch your business transform in ways you never imagined possible.

Cultivating a Proactive Mindset for Growth

One of the most powerful strategies you can adopt is cultivating a proactive mindset. This approach involves anticipating future needs, preparing for upcoming challenges, and seizing opportunities before they become obvious to everyone else.

It's about laying a strong foundation not just for where your business stands today, but for where it could be tomorrow, next year, or even a decade into the future.

The core of a proactive mindset is the anticipation of future trends and challenges. This might mean staying ahead by adopting new technologies, embracing sustainable building practices, or integrating innovative project management techniques.

It involves continuous education for yourself and your team, attending industry conferences, and participating in professional networks. By doing this, you're not just preparing your business for future challenges; you're positioning it to be a pioneer in innovation within your field.

However, being proactive isn't just about foreseeing the future; it's about creating it. This means setting ambitious goals and mapping out actionable steps to achieve them.

It requires regular reviews of your business processes, identifying areas for improvement, and implementing changes before inefficiencies escalate into larger problems.

A proactive leader actively seeks feedback, understanding that growth is an ongoing process demanding constant effort and adjustment.

Fostering a proactive mindset within your business also involves cultivating a culture of accountability and empowerment among your team. Encourage your employees to take initiative, develop innovative solutions, and engage in the decision-making process.

When your team operates from a place of ownership and responsibility, they are more likely to anticipate challenges and address them proactively.

This leads to a more efficient and dynamic business, while also building a stronger, more resilient foundation for future growth.

A proactive mindset is not only beneficial but essential for the growth and sustainability of your contracting business. It's about looking ahead, preparing for the unforeseen, and continually striving for improvement.

By focusing on building a solid foundation first, you're setting your business up for long-term success in an ever-evolving industry.

Remember, the future belongs to those who prepare for it today. Let's start building that future now.

The Power of Positivity in Building Your Contracting Business

Maintaining a positive mindset is not just advantageous—it's essential. The journey of building and growing a business is filled with challenges, setbacks, and occasionally, outright failures.

However, the perspective you bring to these obstacles can make all the difference. This discussion dive into how adopting a positive mindset can help you reach your goals.

Firstly, a positive mindset goes beyond mere optimism; it's about cultivating resilience to navigate tough times. It's the ability to view failures as opportunities for learning and growth rather than as insurmountable barriers.

In the contracting business, where delays, unexpected issues, and changes in plans are common, a positive outlook fuels perseverance. By staying optimistic, you're more likely to remain committed to your goals, devise creative solutions to problems, and ultimately, lead your business toward success.

Positivity also has a ripple effect. It enhances not only your own resilience and productivity but also that of your team.

A leader who confronts challenges with a can-do attitude inspires their team to do the same, fostering a work environment where everyone feels valued and motivated.

A positive work culture attracts clients who are drawn to companies that exude confidence and optimism, as it instills trust in your ability to deliver.

Practicing positivity as a daily habit is crucial. Start by setting realistic goals and celebrating small victories. Encourage open communication within your team, focusing on solutions rather than problems.

Cultivate gratitude by regularly reflecting on your achievements and what you are thankful for. While challenges in business are inevitable, fostering a positive mindset lays a strong foundation for not just surviving but thriving in the competitive world of contracting.

The mindset with which you approach the building and growth of your contracting business can significantly influence its trajectory.

A positive mindset is not an optional extra; it's a critical component of your business's foundation.

By embracing positivity, you'll navigate challenges more effectively and create a thriving business environment that inspires everyone involved—from your team to your clients.

Let positivity be the cornerstone of your contracting business, transforming challenges into stepping stones for success.

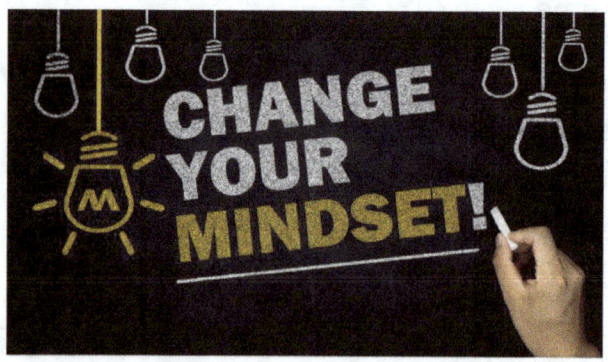

Mindset Matters

When I first started my home improvement business, I was overwhelmed by the sheer enormity of the challenges before me.

The contracting industry is fiercely competitive, and I often found myself bogged down by setbacks and obstacles.

However, everything changed when I began to understand the importance of mindset. I realized that the way I approached my business and personal life was crucial in determining my success.

Adopting a growth mindset, abundant mindset, proactive mindset, and positive mindset became the cornerstones of my transformation.

Embracing a growth mindset was the first pivotal change. I began to see every setback as an opportunity to learn and grow rather than a failure.

For instance, when a project didn't go as planned, instead of dwelling on the loss, I analyzed what went wrong and how I could prevent it in the future.

This shift allowed me to innovate and improve our services continually. I encouraged my team to adopt the same mindset, fostering a culture of continuous learning and development.

This not only improved our work but also strengthened team morale and collaboration.

The abundant mindset taught me the value of collaboration and long-term strategy. I no longer viewed competitors as threats but as potential partners.

This led to collaborations that opened new avenues for growth and success. Planning with a long-term perspective helped me focus on sustainable growth rather than immediate gains.

The proactive mindset prepared me for future challenges, turning potential crises into manageable situations.

And most importantly, a positive mindset fueled my perseverance and inspired my team. This created a work environment that was not only productive but also joyful and fulfilling.

As I continued to build and expand my contracting business, these mindsets served as the pillars supporting my journey.

I realized that success was not solely about the contracts we secured but about the mindset with which we pursued them.

By cultivating these powerful perspectives, I laid the "Foundation First" for a business that is profitable, adaptable, innovative, and enduring.

Chapter Four: Pillar 2: Marketing Systems - The Blueprint for Visibility

Mastering a powerful marketing strategy is not just beneficial—it's crucial.

This chapter aims to shed light on the journey for contracting business owners like you, demonstrating how to attract your ideal clients and significantly grow your business.

The key to this journey lies in understanding that a well-crafted marketing strategy is more than a tool; it is the foundation upon which sustainable growth is constructed.

A successful marketing strategy begins with clarity. Identifying your ideal clients, understanding their needs, and knowing where they spend their time are essential steps.

This clarity enables you to tailor your messaging and services to resonate deeply with them. Think of your marketing strategy as a beacon, one that stands out to your ideal clients amidst a crowded market.

It's about being visible to the right people, in the right places, and at the right times. Employing a blend of traditional and digital marketing tools—from social media platforms to networking events—allows you to cast a wider net while maintaining precision in your targeting.

However, strategy alone isn't sufficient. Execution is what brings it to life. This chapter underscores the importance of consistency, creativity, and measurement.

Regular engagement with your audience through valuable content, staying updated on industry trends, and being innovative in your approach not only enhances your brand presence but also builds trust with potential clients.

Additionally, measuring your marketing efforts is crucial. By analyzing what works and what doesn't, you can make informed decisions and optimize your strategy for better results over time. Remember, a marketing strategy is not static; it's a dynamic blueprint that evolves with your business and the market.

A marketing strategy is your ladder to success. It's about laying a solid foundation upon which your contracting business can securely grow and reach new heights.

Throughout this chapter, we've explored the essential components of creating and implementing a marketing strategy that not only generates leads from your ideal clients but also nurtures these relationships for long-term success.

As you transform these insights into actions, remember that growth is a marathon, not a sprint. With patience, persistence, and a well-crafted marketing strategy, the potential for your business is boundless.

Let this be the foundation upon which your contracting business thrives, achieving new milestones and beyond.

Strategy 1: Digital Presence and SEO

Establishing a strong online presence is no longer optional; it is essential for your success. The majority of your potential clients are actively online, seeking information and services that match their needs.

To capitalize on this, it is crucial to invest in a professional, user-friendly website and prioritize Search Engine Optimization (SEO) strategies. SEO involves optimizing your website so that it ranks higher on search engine results pages (SERPs), making it simpler for potential clients to discover your services.

For instance, consider a local roofing contractor aiming to attract more business. They could optimize their website with targeted keywords that potential clients are likely to use when searching for roofing services.

Keywords such as "best roofing services in [Location]" or "affordable roof repair near me" can significantly increase the site's visibility.

Additionally, creating high-quality content that addresses common roofing issues, showcases past projects, and provides valuable information can help engage visitors and establish credibility.

This strategic approach not only enhances your online visibility but also ensures that the traffic you attract is highly relevant.

By targeting specific, localized search terms, you can reach clients who are actively looking for the services you offer within your geographic area.

This relevance increases the likelihood of converting visitors into leads and, ultimately, paying customers.

Maintaining an active online presence through regular updates, blog posts, and social media engagement can further strengthen your brand's online authority, making it a cornerstone of your overall marketing strategy.

Strategy 2: Social Media and Content Marketing

In today's digital age, social media platforms have evolved far beyond their initial purpose of facilitating social interactions. These platforms have become indispensable tools for businesses aiming to reach and engage with their target audiences effectively.

Leveraging social media for content marketing allows businesses to create and disseminate valuable, relevant information that not only attracts but also retains a clearly defined audience.

By consistently sharing content related to your industry, you position your business as a thought leader and go-to resource, enhancing your brand's credibility and trustworthiness.

For instance, consider a plumbing business. By sharing a variety of content such as tips on maintaining home plumbing systems, step-by-step how-to guides for minor repairs, and case studies showcasing successfully resolved plumbing issues, this business can significantly enhance its online presence.

Platforms like Facebook, Instagram, and LinkedIn provide an ideal space for such content.

On Facebook, the plumbing business can engage with a local community through detailed posts and interactive Q&A sessions.

Instagram, with its visual-centric approach, can be used to post before-and-after photos of plumbing jobs, short video tutorials, and infographics.

LinkedIn, on the other hand, offers a professional environment where the business can share in-depth articles and connect with other professionals in the industry.

This multifaceted approach to social media and content marketing serves multiple purposes. It effectively markets the business's services by showcasing expertise and successful outcomes.

Secondly, it builds a reservoir of trust with the audience. When potential customers see that the business consistently provides valuable, actionable advice, they are more likely to view it as a reliable resource.

This strategy helps in fostering a community of engaged followers who may share the content, further amplifying the business's reach and influence.

This trust translates into a higher likelihood of these individuals choosing the business when they require contracting services.

Strategy 3: Referral Programs

Never underestimate the power of word-of-mouth marketing. Satisfied customers are naturally inclined to recommend your services to their friends, family, and acquaintances.

By implementing a referral program, you can incentivize this organic process, effectively turning your existing clients into enthusiastic advocates for your business.

A well-structured referral program can offer various rewards, such as discounts on future services, gift cards, or even cash bonuses for every successful referral.

This not only encourages your clients to spread the word but also fosters a sense of loyalty and appreciation.

For example, offering a 10% discount on a future service for every new client referred can be a compelling incentive.

This approach capitalizes on the trust and satisfaction your current clients already have, making them more likely to share their positive experiences with others.

The beauty of a referral program is that it leverages the credibility and relationships that your clients have built within their own networks, thereby attracting new clients who are likely to be just as valuable as your existing ones.

This strategy can significantly expand your client base with minimal marketing expenses, as the primary cost is the incentive you offer, which is often offset by the revenue generated from new clients.

Build Your Ideal Client Base

A solid marketing plan and strategy are fundamental for any contracting business aiming for growth.

By leveraging digital marketing, engaging on social media, and encouraging word-of-mouth through well-designed referral programs, you can effectively reach and appeal to your ideal clients.

It's essential to remember that the goal is not just to attract any clients, but the right clients—those who are specifically seeking the services you offer and are likely to become long-term patrons.

With these strategies in place, you set the stage for sustained growth, stability, and success, ensuring that your business thrives in a competitive market.

Identifying and Marketing to Your Ideal Client

Understanding who you are serving is not just beneficial—it's essential for long-term success. Identifying your ideal client is a critical step that can greatly influence your business's growth and sustainability.

This section dives into the significance of pinpointing your ideal client and explores how this knowledge can become the cornerstone for your business's strategic planning and marketing efforts.

First and foremost, knowing your ideal client helps you tailor your marketing strategies more effectively.

When you have a clear picture of the demographics, preferences, and pain points of your target audience, you can create highly targeted marketing campaigns.

These campaigns are more likely to resonate with potential clients, leading to higher engagement rates and better conversion outcomes.

For instance, if your ideal client values eco-friendly solutions, emphasizing sustainable practices in your marketing materials can help you connect on a deeper level.

Understanding your ideal client allows you to refine your service offerings to meet specific needs. By focusing on what your target market truly desires, you can develop specialized services that set you apart from competitors.

This not only enhances client satisfaction but also fosters loyalty, turning one-time customers into repeat clients and brand advocates.

Additionally, word-of-mouth recommendations from satisfied clients can serve as powerful, organic marketing tools, further expanding your reach.

Identifying your ideal client is a foundational element for any contracting business. It enables you to deploy more effective marketing strategies and refine your service offerings, ensuring that you meet the unique needs of your target market.

By investing time and resources into understanding your ideal client, you establish a solid foundation for sustainable growth and long-term success in a competitive industry.

Identifying Your Ideal Client

The first step in this crucial process is to identify who your ideal client is. This is not about casting a wide net and hoping for the best but rather about precision and strategic focus.

Begin by analyzing your past projects to gather insights. Which ones were the most successful in terms of outcomes and client satisfaction? Which clients were a joy to work with, and which projects were the most profitable?

These questions can help you paint a detailed picture of your ideal client.

Consider various factors such as the type of projects (residential, commercial, industrial, etc.), the project size and scope, the geographical location, and even the client's personality and communication style.

For instance, do you prefer working with clients who have a clear vision and are decisive, or do you enjoy collaborating with those who value creative input and flexibility?

By creating a comprehensive client profile, you essentially set a standard that will guide your business in attracting the right kind of projects.

This profile should include demographic information such as age, income level, and industry, as well as psychographic details like values, interests, and pain points.

Also, think about the long-term potential of these clients: Are they likely to provide repeat business or refer you to others within their network? The more specific you can be, the better.

This detailed understanding will serve as a foundation for all subsequent marketing and business development efforts, ensuring that your resources are directed towards the most promising opportunities.

Marketing to Your Ideal Client

Once you've identified your ideal client, the next step is to tailor your marketing efforts to speak directly to them.

This involves crafting your messaging, visuals, and overall branding to resonate with the specific needs and desires of your target market.

Start with a compelling value proposition that clearly outlines how your services can solve their problems or meet their needs. Utilize social media platforms like LinkedIn, Instagram, or Facebook to engage with your audience and showcase your expertise.

Your business website should be optimized to highlight your experience in handling projects that align with your ideal client's preferences.

This includes creating dedicated landing pages, blog posts, and resource sections that address common questions and concerns.

Traditional marketing materials such as brochures, flyers, and business cards should also reflect your focus on your ideal client.

Use testimonials, case studies, and portfolio pieces to illustrate your capability and success in projects similar to those your ideal client is likely to undertake.

Visual content like before-and-after photos, video walkthroughs, and client interviews can be particularly effective in building trust and credibility.

Also, consider hosting webinars, workshops, or networking events to provide value and establish yourself as a thought leader in your industry.

By consistently delivering content and experiences that resonate with your ideal client, you not only attract them but also foster long-term relationships that contribute to sustained business growth.

The Overlooked Marketing Goldmine- Past Clients and Your Business Growth

While it's important to continuously expand your client base, one of the most powerful yet often overlooked strategies is marketing to your past clients.

These individuals have already experienced your work, and maintaining a relationship with them can lead to repeat business, referrals, and a robust reputation in your community.

Early in my home improvement business, I was so focused on finding new clients that I neglected the ones I had already served.

I assumed that once a project was completed, the relationship with the client was over. My calendar was packed with marketing initiatives targeting new prospects, and I rarely followed up with past clients.

It wasn't until I experienced a significant downturn in business that I realized the importance of nurturing these existing relationships.

Growth Through Your Ideal Client

Understanding and targeting your ideal client does more than just attract business—it lays a robust foundation for sustainable growth.

When you work with clients that fit your ideal profile, projects tend to run smoother, satisfaction rates are higher, and the likelihood of repeat business and referrals increases.

This creates a cycle of positive word-of-mouth, expanding your client base with more of your ideal clients. As you consistently deliver exceptional results to those who truly value your services, you build a reputation for reliability and excellence.

Working with your ideal clients also allows you to hone your skills in specific areas, enhancing your expertise and reputation in the market.

This specialization can make your business the go-to contractor for specific types of projects, significantly contributing to your business's growth and success.

By focusing on a niche where you excel, you become a trusted authority, which not only sets you apart from competitors but also attracts a more discerning clientele willing to pay a premium for your specialized knowledge and experience.

The Ideal Client Advantage

Identifying and marketing to your ideal client is not just a strategy; it's a foundational element of building and growing your contracting business.

By understanding who your ideal client is, you can align your business practices, marketing efforts, and project execution to meet their needs, resulting in a more focused, efficient, and profitable business.

Tailoring your approach to resonate with your ideal clients means you're not wasting resources on less suitable prospects, allowing you to concentrate on delivering value where it's most appreciated.

Remember, when you know who you're looking for, finding them—and serving them well—becomes much easier.

This well-targeted focus leads to a stronger, more resilient business model, where client satisfaction and loyalty drive sustained growth and long-term success.

By shifting my focus to maintaining contact with my past clients, I began to see substantial improvements in repeat business and referrals, which, in turn, stabilized and grew my company.

Here are three invaluable tips on how to keep in touch with your past clients to grow your business:

1. **Regular Follow-Ups:**
   After completing a project, make it a habit to check in with your clients periodically. This could be a simple phone call, an email, or even a handwritten note. Ask them how the project is holding up and if there's anything more you can do for them. This not only shows that you care about their satisfaction but also keeps you top-of-mind for any future needs they might have.
2. **Special Offers and Updates:**
   Send your past clients exclusive offers or updates about new services and products. Whether it's a seasonal discount or a sneak peek at a new home improvement trend, these communications can prompt them to consider new projects or recommend your services to friends and family.

3. **Engage on Social Media:**
   Social media is a powerful tool for maintaining relationships. Encourage your past clients to follow your business on platforms like Facebook and Instagram. Share updates, success stories, and tips that can help them maintain their homes. Engaging with their posts and responding to their comments can further strengthen your relationship and keep your business visible in their daily lives.

By focusing on building and maintaining relationships with your past clients, you not only create a loyal customer base but also generate a solid stream of referrals and repeat business.

This strategy not only helps in reaching your business goals but also fosters a community of satisfied clients who trust and value your work.

As I learned from my own experience, the time and effort invested in keeping up with past clients can significantly contribute to the long-term success and growth of your home improvement business.

From Struggle to Success- How Strategic Marketing Transformed My Business

In the early days of my contracting business, I faced a multitude of challenges. Despite my relentless efforts, I struggled to keep a steady stream of clients.

The inconsistency in work was discouraging, and I knew I needed a more effective approach to ensure the survival and growth of my business.

That's when I decided to dive into the intricacies of marketing, focusing on strategies that would specifically target my ideal clients. The transformation that followed was nothing short of remarkable.

The first step in this journey was identifying and understanding my ideal client. I realized that a one-size-fits-all marketing approach was futile.

By zeroing in on the specific needs, preferences, and pain points of my target demographic, I could tailor my marketing messages to resonate deeply with them.

I conducted extensive research, engaged in conversations, and gathered feedback to create a detailed profile of my ideal client.

This clarity enabled me to craft marketing campaigns that spoke directly to them, addressing their specific concerns and offering tailored solutions.

The precision of this approach not only increased the chances of converting prospects into clients but also ensured that my marketing resources were used efficiently.

Building a robust digital presence was the next crucial step. I revamped my website, ensuring it was optimized for search engines and user-friendly.

By targeting localized search terms, I was able to attract clients who were actively seeking the services I offered within my geographic area.

Regular updates, blog posts, and social media engagement further strengthened my online visibility.

Platforms like Facebook and Instagram became invaluable tools for disseminating valuable content and engaging with my audience.

This not only positioned my business as a thought leader but also built trust and credibility.

The consistency in my digital marketing efforts paid off, as I began to see a steady increase in inquiries and bookings.

However, the real game-changer was leveraging the power of word-of-mouth marketing and nurturing relationships with past clients.

Early on, I made the mistake of neglecting clients once a project was completed. Realizing this oversight, I shifted my focus to maintaining contact with past clients through regular follow-ups, exclusive offers, and social media engagement.

This approach fostered loyalty and led to repeat business and referrals.

The impact on my business was profound; not only did it stabilize my workload, but it also set the stage for sustainable growth.

By strategically targeting my ideal clients and maintaining strong relationships, I was able to transform my struggling business into a thriving enterprise.

Chapter FIVE: Pillar 3: Sales Systems - Constructing the Deal

Having a powerful sales system isn't just a luxury—it's an essential pillar of your contracting business.

This chapter dives into the critical role a well-structured sales system plays in your business and how it can serve as the foundation of sustainable growth and success.

At the core of an effective sales system is its power to streamline operations, nurture customer relationships, and drive revenue.

Key components include lead nurturing, diligent follow-up, in-home sales, and exceptional customer service.

Lead nurturing ensures that potential clients are attentively guided through the sales funnel, boosting the chances of conversion.

Consistent follow-up keeps your business at the forefront of prospects' minds and demonstrates unwavering commitment.

In-home sales offer a personalized touch, enabling your team to address client concerns and showcase your offerings directly.

Exceptional customer service fortifies relationships and fosters loyalty, leading to repeat business and valuable referrals.

Integrating these elements into your sales process promises consistency, enhances efficiency, and enriches the overall customer experience.

By embracing a structured and thorough sales approach, your business can significantly amplify its profitability and influence.

Investing in training and development empowers your team to convey value effectively and forge strong connections with potential clients.

Leveraging technology, such as sales automation tools, streamlines lead management, tracks progress, and analyzes performance, freeing your team to focus on high-impact tasks.

Continuously refining your sales strategies based on market feedback keeps your business ahead of the competition and attuned to evolving client needs.

Ultimately, a meticulously honed sales system acts as the engine driving your business forward, laying a solid foundation for growth, profitability, and sustained success.

In the world of business, selling effectively is as crucial as delivering exceptional projects. Let your sales system be the cornerstone of your business's stellar reputation.

Providing Exceptional Customer Service to Elevate Your Contracting Business

Customer service is not just a department; it's the backbone of your business. Building a profitable business relies heavily on the satisfaction and loyalty of your clients.

Exceptional customer service can set you apart from competitors, create repeat business, and generate positive word-of-mouth referrals.

This section will dive into the essential elements of providing exceptional customer service and how these practices can help you build a loyal customer base.

Communication is Key

One of the most critical aspects of customer service is communication. From the moment a client contacts you for a quote until the final brushstroke is applied, keeping your clients informed is paramount.

Let your clients know what to expect and when to expect it. Clearly outline the steps of your process, providing timelines and any necessary preparations they need to make.

If there are any delays or changes, communicate them promptly and professionally.

This level of transparency builds trust and reassures clients that they are in capable hands.

Be Respectful and Attentive

Respect is the foundation of any successful relationship, and this principle holds true in customer service.

Always treat your clients with respect and dignity. Listen to their concerns attentively and address them promptly.

If you make a mistake, own up to it, apologize sincerely, and take immediate steps to rectify the situation.

Demonstrating accountability shows clients that you value their satisfaction and are committed to delivering high-quality service.

Attention to Detail

Attention to detail can make or break your reputation. Ensure that your work is neat and clean, taking care to protect your client's property from any damage. Small details, like covering furniture and flooring, can make a significant difference in the client's experience.

Offer options and recommendations tailored to your client's needs and budget. By providing expert advice and multiple choices, you empower clients to make informed decisions that best suit their preferences.

Punctuality and Professionalism

Time is a valuable resource, and showing respect for your client's time is a mark of professionalism. Always be punctual for appointments and project timelines. If unforeseen delays occur, inform your client as soon as possible.

Alongside punctuality, maintain a professional demeanor at all times. Dress appropriately, use proper language, and act courteously. Your professional behavior reflects the quality of your business and helps build a positive impression.

Be responsive to customer inquiries and concerns throughout the project. Prompt responses make clients feel valued and heard, fostering a sense of trust and reliability.

Providing Value and Building Relationships

Ultimately, providing exceptional customer service is about offering value and building lasting relationships.

Offer competitive pricing without compromising on the quality of your work.

Go above and beyond to exceed your client's expectations, creating memorable experiences that encourage them to return for future projects and recommend your services to others.

Focus on building long-term relationships by maintaining open lines of communication and consistently delivering excellent service.

By adhering to these principles, you can transform your business into a customer-centric enterprise that thrives on loyalty and positive referrals.

Exceptional customer service is not just about meeting expectations; it's about exceeding them and creating a foundation of trust and satisfaction that will support the growth and success of your business.

Nurturing Leads - The Lifeblood of Your Home Improvement Business

In the competitive world of home improvement, leads are the lifeblood of your business. However, generating leads is only the first step; the real art lies in nurturing them.

This section dives into the importance of having an effective lead nurturing system and how it can positively impact your business, building immense value over time.

Understanding Lead Nurturing

Lead nurturing is the process of developing relationships with potential customers at every stage of the sales funnel and through every step of the buyer's journey.

It focuses on listening to the needs of prospects and providing the information and answers they need.

The goal is to build trust, educate, and keep your business top-of-mind until the prospect is ready to make a purchase.

An effective lead nurturing system can transform casual inquiries into loyal customers.

Imagine a homeowner who fills out a form on your website expressing interest in a kitchen remodel.

Without a nurturing system, this lead could easily go cold. However, with a structured follow-up process, you can send them valuable content such as design ideas, testimonials, and even a personalized consultation offer.

This shows the prospect that you're not just interested in making a sale, but in providing value and understanding their specific needs.

The Benefits of Lead Nurturing

1. **Increased Conversion Rates:**
   A nurtured lead is more likely to convert into a paying customer. According to research, nurtured leads make 47% larger purchases than non-nurtured leads. By providing relevant and consistent communication, you keep prospects engaged, making them more likely to choose your services when they're ready to move forward with their home improvement project.

2. **Building Trust and Credibility:**
   In the home improvement industry, trust is paramount. Homeowners need to feel confident that they are hiring professionals who are reliable and skilled. By offering well-crafted content that addresses their concerns and showcases your expertise, you build credibility. This could be in the form of blog posts, case studies, how-to videos, or even just timely responses to their inquiries.

3. **Long-term Relationship Building**:
   Lead nurturing is not just about short-term gains; it's about creating long-lasting relationships. A homeowner who feels valued and informed is more likely to come back for future projects and refer your services to others. This ongoing relationship can lead to repeat business and a steady stream of referrals, which are invaluable for sustained growth.

Implementing a Lead Nurturing System

To implement a successful lead nurturing system, start by segmenting your leads based on their behaviors and interests.

Use customer relationship management (CRM) tools to track interactions and tailor your communications accordingly.

Create a calendar for regular follow-ups, and use a mix of emails, phone calls, and content marketing to keep your leads engaged.

Personalization is key—address your leads by name and reference their specific interests or inquiries.

Automation can be a powerful tool. Automated email sequences, for example, can ensure that no lead falls through the cracks.

However, balance automation with personal touches to avoid coming across as impersonal or robotic.

Nurturing leads is not just an optional strategy; it's a critical component of building a profitable home improvement business.

By investing time and resources into a structured lead nurturing system, you can significantly increase your conversion rates, build lasting trust and credibility, and foster long-term relationships that drive sustained growth.

Remember, the foundation of your business is not just built on the projects you complete but on the relationships you nurture along the way.

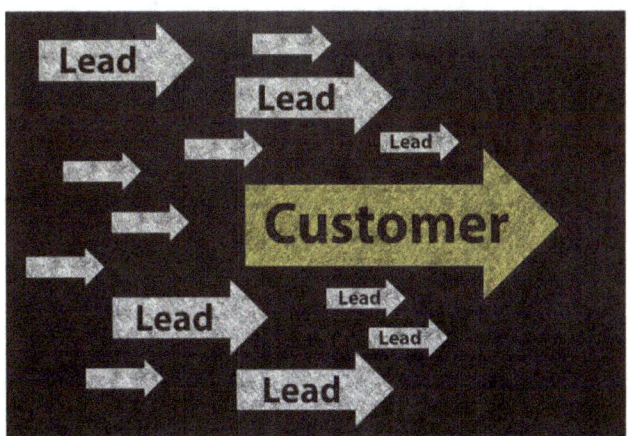

The Art of Upselling: Elevating Your Sales Process

Introduction to Upselling

In the competitive world of home improvement, standing out isn't just about offering exceptional services; it's about maximizing every opportunity that comes your way.

This is where the art of upselling comes into play.

Upselling isn't merely a tactic to increase sales; it's a strategic approach to building deeper customer relationships and delivering enhanced value.

When done correctly, upselling can transform your home improvement business into a profitable powerhouse, creating loyal customers who appreciate the added value.

The Power of an Upselling System

Implementing a structured upselling system within your sales process can profoundly impact your bottom line.

An upselling system ensures that every interaction with a potential customer is optimized to explore additional needs and offer relevant upgrades.

This systematic approach involves training your sales team to identify opportunities, present them effectively, and ensure customers understand the benefits.

Understanding the Concept of Upselling

Upselling is a strategic approach to encourage customers to purchase additional services or higher-end products than they initially planned.

For home improvement business owners, like you, mastering the art of upselling can lead to significant business growth and increased customer satisfaction.

The key is to provide value through quality enhancements and additional services that genuinely benefit the client.

Step-by-Step Approach to Effective Upselling

1. **Know Your Customers' Needs:**
   To effectively upsell, you must first understand your customers' needs and preferences. Conduct thorough consultations to learn about their primary goals, budget constraints, and any specific concerns they might have about the project. This information will help you tailor your upselling strategies to align with their desires and financial capabilities.

2. **Offer Value-Added Services:**
   Identify services that complement the primary project. For instance, if a client is renovating their kitchen, suggest adding energy-efficient appliances or smart home integrations. When proposing these additional services, emphasize the long-term benefits, such as cost savings on utility bills or increased home value. Always ensure that the upsell enhances the overall project and delivers tangible value.

3. **Present Premium Options**:
Offer premium materials or advanced technologies as upgrades. For example, if a customer is installing new flooring, present the benefits of opting for hardwood over laminate. Highlight the durability, aesthetic appeal, and potential return on investment of the premium choice. Use visual aids, such as samples or before-and-after photos, to make a compelling case.

Techniques to Enhance Upselling Success

1. **Build Trust and Credibility**:
Customers are more likely to consider upsells from a business they trust. Foster credibility by showcasing your expertise, sharing positive testimonials, and providing transparent pricing. Demonstrating a genuine commitment to quality and customer satisfaction will make clients more receptive to your suggestions.

2. **Create Package Deals**:
   Design bundled packages that offer a combination of services at a discounted rate. This approach not only makes the upsell more attractive but also simplifies the decision-making process for the customer. For instance, a complete bathroom remodel package could include plumbing upgrades, new fixtures, and custom cabinetry at a competitive price.

3. **Train Your Team**:
   Ensure that your sales and project management teams are well-versed in upselling techniques. Provide ongoing training on product knowledge, customer service, and effective communication. A knowledgeable and confident team can seamlessly integrate upselling into their interactions with clients, leading to higher success rates.

Monitoring and Adapting Your Strategies

Regularly review the effectiveness of your upselling efforts by tracking metrics such as conversion rates, average transaction value, and customer feedback.

Use this data to refine your strategies, identify areas for improvement, and celebrate successful outcomes. Staying adaptable and responsive to market trends and customer preferences will keep your upselling approach relevant and impactful.

Building Value Through Upselling

Upselling isn't just about increasing the sales ticket; it's about enhancing the overall customer experience.

When customers feel they are getting more value, they are more likely to trust your recommendations and perceive your business as a premium service provider.

This perception can lead to repeat business, positive reviews, and referrals, all of which are invaluable for sustained growth.

An effective upselling strategy can differentiate your business from competitors. By offering tailored solutions that address specific customer needs, you demonstrate a higher level of expertise and commitment to quality.

For example, offering a package deal that includes a home energy audit with every major renovation project can set you apart as a leader in comprehensive home improvement solutions.

Implementing Your Upselling System

To successfully integrate upselling into your sales process, start by training your team on the importance of understanding customer needs.

Equip them with the knowledge of various products and services that complement the primary offerings.

Role-playing scenarios can be an effective training tool, helping your team practice how to introduce upgrades naturally and persuasively.

For instance, if you're installing new windows, your sales team can suggest energy-efficient models that may cost more upfront but save the customer in the long run.

By presenting these options as value additions rather than mere upsells, customers are more likely to see the merit in investing a bit more.

This not only increases immediate sales but also positions your business as one that genuinely cares about customer satisfaction and long-term savings.

The Benefits of an In-Home Sales Process

The in-home sales process stands out as a powerful tool for growth, profitability, and goal achievement.

This personalized approach not only allows for a detailed presentation of your services but also facilitates a deeper connection with potential customers.

By following a structured in-home sales process, you can significantly enhance your business outcomes.

Building Trust and Rapport

One of the primary benefits of an in-home sales process is the opportunity to build trust and rapport with potential customers.

When you set up an appointment and meet clients in their own space, you demonstrate a level of professionalism and commitment that can be hard to convey through other sales methods.

Dressing professionally and arriving prepared with materials such as paint samples, brochures, and a portfolio of previous work showcases your dedication and attention to detail.

This personal interaction helps to humanize your business, making customers more likely to trust you and feel comfortable discussing their needs and preferences.

Enhancing Customer Satisfaction and Closing Rates

An in-home sales presentation allows you to tailor your pitch to the specific needs of each customer.

By assessing their requirements and showing them relevant examples from your portfolio, you can make a strong case for why your services are the best fit for their project.

Providing samples for them to view in their own lighting conditions further enhances their decision-making process.

Discussing pricing transparently and addressing any questions or concerns they may have helps to eliminate uncertainties.

This customized approach not only increases the likelihood of closing deals but also ensures higher customer satisfaction, as clients feel their specific needs are being met.

Driving Business Growth and Profitability

Implementing a well-executed in-home sales process can have a significant impact on your business growth and profitability.

By consistently closing more deals, you can boost your revenue and expand your customer base.

Additionally, the positive experiences of satisfied customers can lead to valuable word-of-mouth referrals, further driving business growth.

The personal touch of an in-home presentation often makes clients more willing to invest in higher-quality services, thereby increasing your average transaction value.

Following up after the meeting to confirm job details and address any remaining questions reinforces your commitment to customer service, further solidifying your reputation and encouraging repeat business.

Achieving Long-Term Goals

Ultimately, the in-home sales process is not just about closing individual sales; it's about building a sustainable business model that supports your long-term goals.

By establishing a reliable method for engaging with customers and consistently delivering high-quality service, you create a strong foundation for your business.

This approach enables you to set and achieve ambitious targets, whether it's expanding your service area, increasing your team size, or launching new product offerings.

The trust and rapport built through in-home presentations can lead to long-term relationships with clients, providing a steady stream of projects and income.

Implementing the In-Home Sales Process

Now that we've explored the numerous benefits of an in-home sales process, let's dive into the practical steps to implement this strategy effectively in your business.

Transitioning to or refining an in-home sales approach requires careful planning and execution to ensure that you maximize its potential.

Step 1: Preparation and Scheduling

Before you set foot in a potential customer's home, thorough preparation is key.

Begin by scheduling your appointments efficiently, ensuring you have ample time between visits to avoid rushing.

When booking the appointment, gather as much information as possible about the customer's needs, preferences, and any specific concerns they might have. This will allow you to tailor your presentation accordingly.

Step 2: Presentation Materials

Having the right materials on hand is essential to making a compelling case for your services.

Create a professional portfolio showcasing your best work, including before-and-after photos, customer testimonials, and detailed descriptions of previous projects.

Additionally, prepare a range of samples and brochures that illustrate the variety of options available. Ensure your materials are well-organized and easily accessible during your presentation.

Step 3: Professional Appearance and Conduct

First impressions matter, so dress professionally and arrive on time.

Greet your potential customers warmly and respectfully, making them feel at ease. Your demeanor should reflect confidence without arrogance, and you should be ready to listen actively to their needs and concerns.

Building a genuine connection from the outset can significantly influence the outcome of your sales pitch.

Step 4: Customized Pitch and Demonstration

Tailor your presentation to the specific needs of the customer. Walk through their space with them, discussing their vision and providing expert recommendations.

Use your portfolio to highlight similar projects and explain how your services can meet their unique requirements.

Offer hands-on demonstrations with paint samples, allowing customers to see and feel the quality of your materials in their own environment.

Step 5: Transparent Pricing and Proposal

Discuss pricing transparently, providing a detailed proposal that explains costs and outlines the scope of the project.

Be prepared to answer any questions they may have and address concerns about budget, timeline, and project execution.

Transparency builds trust and helps prevent misunderstandings later in the process.

Step 6: Closing the deal

One of the standout advantages of an in-home sales process is the ability to close deals on the spot.

Unlike sending over a proposal and waiting for a response, conducting the consultation in person allows for immediate feedback and decision-making.

During the in-home consultation, you can address any final concerns or objections the customer might have, providing real-time solutions and adjustments to your proposal.

This immediacy can be the difference between a potential client choosing your services or continuing to shop around.

Step 7: Follow-Up and Customer Engagement

After the initial meeting, follow up promptly to reinforce your commitment to their project. Send a thank-you note or email, reiterating key points from your discussion and expressing your enthusiasm for the opportunity to work with them.

This follow-up not only keeps the lines of communication open but also demonstrates your dedication to customer service.

Step 8: Ongoing Relationship Management

The in-home sales process doesn't end once the deal is closed. Maintain regular contact with your customers throughout the project, providing updates and addressing any issues that arise.

After the project is completed, reach out to ensure their satisfaction and to request feedback.

Happy customers are more likely to provide referrals and repeat business, so nurturing these relationships is crucial.

By following these steps, you can implement an in-home sales process that not only boosts your business but also enhances the customer experience.

As you refine your approach and adapt to the unique needs of each client, you'll find that this personalized method sets you apart in the competitive painting industry, driving both immediate and long-term success.

The Power of Persistence: Follow-Up as Your Sales System's Backbone

Setting your business apart goes beyond just delivering quality work; it involves building enduring relationships with your clients through a robust follow-up system.

This section dives into the importance of follow-up as an indispensable tool in building your profitable business.

By weaving follow-up into the fabric of your sales strategy, you not only enhance customer satisfaction but also lay a solid foundation for sustainable growth and profitability.

Follow-up, when consistently applied, serves as a powerful tool to keep your business at the forefront of clients' minds, turning one-time projects into long-term partnerships.

This persistence in communication demonstrates your commitment to excellence and client satisfaction, fostering a sense of trust and reliability.

It opens avenues for receiving valuable feedback, enabling you to refine your services and address any concerns promptly.

This proactive approach significantly contributes to a positive reputation, which is instrumental in attracting new projects through word-of-mouth and repeat business.

Also, by maintaining regular contact, you are better positioned to anticipate client needs and offer solutions before they turn to competitors, thereby increasing your market share and profitability.

Implementing an effective follow-up strategy in your business can be achieved through various methods, each tailored to different stages of the customer journey.

Here are three practical ways to follow up with leads and nurture them into loyal clients:

1. **The Personalized Email**:
   After an initial meeting or inquiry, send a personalized email thanking the potential client for considering your services. Highlight key points discussed and reiterate how your business can address their specific needs. This not only shows professionalism but also reinforces the value you bring to their project.
2. **The Check-In Call**:
   A week or two after sending your proposal, follow up with a phone call to answer any questions they might have. This direct form of communication can clarify any uncertainties and gives you an opportunity to further solidify your relationship with the potential client. It's a chance to demonstrate your enthusiasm for their project and your commitment to providing exceptional service.

3. **The Value-Added Follow-Up**: Beyond just checking in, provide additional value with each interaction. This could be in the form of sharing a relevant case study, offering a complimentary consultation to further discuss their project needs, or sending a brief newsletter with insights relevant to their business or industry. This strategy not only keeps the communication lines open but also showcases your expertise and dedication to adding value at every opportunity.

Integrating follow-up as a core component of your sales system is not merely about staying in touch; it's about building trust, demonstrating value, and creating lasting relationships that drive profitability.

By adopting these follow-up strategies, you position your contracting business as a trusted advisor and partner, paving the way for growth and success in a competitive marketplace.

From Good to Great: Enhancing Business Profits Through Superior Customer Service"

When I started on my journey to enhance my business profits and clientele, I quickly realized that exceptional customer service was the key to success.

I was determined to stand out in a competitive market by ensuring every interaction with my clients was memorable and positive.

This meant transforming customer service from a mere department into the backbone of my business.

I began by focusing on clear and consistent communication, setting expectations from the initial contact to the project's completion. By keeping clients informed about every step, from timelines to any changes that arose, I built a foundation of trust and reliability.

This transparency reassured my clients that their projects were in capable hands, which in turn fostered loyalty and repeat business.

Respect and attention to detail became my guiding principles.

I treated every client with the utmost respect, listening to their concerns attentively and addressing them promptly.

When mistakes occurred, I didn't shy away from owning them, apologizing sincerely, and taking immediate steps to rectify the situation.

This accountability demonstrated my commitment to their satisfaction and reinforced my dedication to delivering high-quality service.

I also paid meticulous attention to every detail of my work, ensuring that the client's property was protected and that the final outcome exceeded their expectations.

Small gestures, such as covering furniture and flooring, made a significant difference in the client's experience, solidifying my reputation for excellence.

Implementing an effective follow-up strategy significantly contributed to my success.

After an initial meeting or inquiry, I sent personalized emails thanking potential clients for considering my services and reiterating how I could meet their specific needs.

A week or two after sending a proposal, I made follow-up phone calls to answer any questions and further solidify relationships.

Adding value with each interaction, whether by sharing relevant project information or offering complimentary consultations, kept communication lines open and showcased my expertise.

This proactive approach not only increased my closing rates but also built long-term relationships with clients, leading to higher repeat business and positive word-of-mouth referrals.

By transforming my customer service practices and focusing on relationship-building, I was able to elevate my sales process, sell at higher rates, and significantly increase my profits.

Chapter SIX: Pillar 4: Knowing Your Numbers - The Financial Framework

Understanding the financial underpinnings of your business is not just important—it's essential.

This chapter, "Knowing Your Numbers," is designed to serve as a pillar for contractors aspiring to not only build but significantly grow their business.

It's about laying a foundation so solid that every decision made is informed, every risk calculated, and every opportunity maximized for profitability.

We will focus particularly on Lifetime Client Value, average project size, profit margin, business and personal financial goals, and effective project pricing.

Knowing your numbers goes far beyond simply keeping track of income and expenses. It involves a deep understanding of how various financial metrics interrelate and impact your overall business health.

For instance, Lifetime Client Value (LCV) is a crucial metric that informs you of the total revenue you can expect from a customer over the duration of your relationship.

By maximizing LCV through exceptional service and strategic upselling, you can secure a steady revenue stream that supports long-term growth.

Similarly, understanding the average project size helps you forecast income, allocate resources efficiently, and plan for future projects more effectively.

Profit margin is another critical area where precision is paramount. By carefully calculating and monitoring your profit margins, you can ensure that your pricing strategies are not only competitive but also sustainable.

This ties directly into setting both business and personal financial goals, which provide a roadmap for growth and success.

Effective project pricing, informed by a thorough understanding of these metrics, ensures that you cover costs while still offering value to your clients.

Mastering these elements can be the difference between a flourishing business and one that struggles to keep its head above water.

Knowing your numbers empowers you to make informed decisions, optimize operations, and achieve financial stability, thereby laying the groundwork for lasting success.

Let this chapter be the foundation upon which you build a business that not only survives but thrives in the ever-evolving landscape of contracting.

Setting the Right Price - The Keystone of Your Business Foundation

Pricing your projects accurately ensures you cover all your costs and make a significant profit.

This profit is essential for reinvesting in your business, paying yourself and your team fairly, and funding your growth initiatives.

When you price too low, you may win more projects, but you risk eroding your profitability, leading to cash flow problems and an inability to invest in high-quality materials or skilled labor.

Conversely, pricing too high can deter potential clients and reduce the number of projects you secure.

Tips for Pricing at a 50% Gross Profit Margin

1. **Know Your Costs:**
   Begin by understanding your direct and indirect costs. Direct costs include materials and labor directly associated with the project, while indirect costs cover overheads like rent, utilities, and administrative expenses. Ensure you account for all these costs to avoid underpricing.

2. **Calculate Your Markup:**
   To achieve a 50% gross profit margin, you need to mark up your costs by 100%. For example, if your total costs for a project amount to $5,000, you should price the project at $10,000. This ensures that $5,000 covers your costs, and the remaining $5,000 is your gross profit.

3. **Market Research:**
   Understand your market and what your competitors are charging for similar projects. While it's important to stay competitive, don't undervalue your services. Highlight the unique value and quality you bring to justify your pricing.

4. **Transparent Pricing:**
   Be transparent with your clients about your pricing structure. Explain the value and quality they are receiving, which helps in building trust and justifying your prices. Clients are often willing to pay more for a project when they understand the benefits and quality they are receiving.

5. **Regular Review:**
   Periodically review and adjust your pricing strategy to reflect changes in costs, market conditions, and business goals. This ensures you remain profitable and competitive over time.

Impact on Your Business and Goals

Pricing your projects for a 50% gross profit margin has a profound impact on your business's health and your ability to achieve your goals.

Higher profitability means more resources for marketing, hiring skilled workers, and investing in better tools and materials.

It enables you to take on more significant projects and expansions, enhancing your reputation and market presence.

A healthy pricing strategy translates to better financial stability, allowing you to weather economic downturns and unexpected expenses more effectively.

It also provides the funds necessary for continuous learning and development, keeping you ahead in an ever-evolving industry.

By prioritizing a strong foundation through accurate and strategic pricing, you set your home improvement business on a path to sustainable growth and success.

It's not just about winning projects; it's about winning the right projects at the right price, ensuring profitability and achieving your long-term objectives.

Understanding Your Profit Margin

Knowing your profit margin isn't just about keeping your business afloat; it's the compass that guides your company towards sustainable growth and success.

Understanding Profit Margins

Profit margins are a critical metric for any home improvement business owner. They reflect the percentage of revenue that exceeds the costs of providing your services.

Essentially, your profit margin represents how much money you're making for every dollar you bring in.

To calculate your profit margin, you need to subtract your total expenses from your total revenue and then divide that number by your total revenue. Finally, multiply by 100 to get a percentage. The formula looks like this:

[{Profit Margin} = ({Total Revenue} - {Total Expenses}{Total Revenue}) \times 100]

Tips to Increase Profit Margins

1. **Streamline Operations:**
   Evaluate your current operations to identify inefficiencies. This might involve adopting new technologies, improving workflow processes, or investing in employee training. Efficient operations reduce costs and increase the gap between revenue and expenses.
2. **Negotiate with Suppliers:**
   Building good relationships with your suppliers can lead to better prices or more favorable payment terms. Don't hesitate to negotiate for bulk discounts or explore alternative suppliers who can offer better deals.

3. **Value-Based Pricing**:
   Instead of competing solely on price, focus on the value you provide. Highlight the quality of your work, your expertise, and the benefits your customers receive. When clients understand the value, they are often willing to pay a premium.
4. **Reduce Waste**:
   In home improvement, materials can often go to waste. Implement better inventory management to reduce excess and ensure that materials are used efficiently. Reusing and recycling materials can also cut down costs.
5. **Upsell and Cross-Sell**:
   Train your team to identify opportunities to offer additional services or upgrades to customers. For instance, if a customer is getting their kitchen remodeled, you might suggest complementary services like a new backsplash or custom cabinetry.

Impact on Your Business and Goals

Increasing your profit margins can have a profound impact on your business. Higher profit margins mean more money can be reinvested into the business, allowing for expansion, better equipment, and more skilled labor.

It also means greater financial stability, making it easier to weather economic downturns or unexpected expenses.

Furthermore, healthier profit margins can help you achieve your long-term business goals.

Whether you're looking to expand geographically, diversify your service offerings, or simply ensure a more comfortable personal income, focusing on profit margins puts you in a stronger position to make those dreams a reality.

By maintaining a keen eye on your profits and continuously seeking ways to improve them, you lay a solid foundation for sustained business growth and success.

Setting and Achieving Your Business and Personal Financial Goals

Establishing clear and attainable financial goals is a cornerstone for any successful home improvement business.

Whether you're aiming to expand your services, hire additional staff, or simply increase your profit margins, setting precise goals provides a roadmap for your business's future.

Aligning your business goals with personal financial aspirations ensures that your entrepreneurial journey supports your broader life ambitions.

Calculating Your Goals

To begin, you must understand where your business currently stands financially.

This involves a thorough analysis of your current revenue, expenses, and profit margins. Utilize accounting software or consult with a financial advisor to get an accurate snapshot of your financial health.

Once you have this baseline, you can set specific, measurable, achievable, relevant, and time-bound (SMART) goals. For example, if your annual revenue is $500,000 and you aim to increase it by 20% over the next year, your target revenue would be $600,000.

Next, break down this annual goal into quarterly and monthly targets. This makes the goal more manageable and allows for regular progress checks.

For instance, reaching a $600,000 annual revenue target means hitting approximately $50,000 in monthly revenue. These smaller increments make it easier to adjust strategies and operations as needed.

Reaching Your Goals

Once your goals are clearly defined, developing a strategic plan to achieve them is essential. This might involve investing in new tools or technology, enhancing your marketing efforts, or increasing your workforce.

Generate a detailed action plan that outlines the steps needed to reach each milestone. For instance, if increasing monthly revenue requires acquiring more clients, you might allocate a budget for enhanced online advertising or develop partnerships with local real estate firms.

Accountability is a crucial component in reaching your goals. Regularly review your progress towards your financial targets and adjust your strategies as necessary.

Establishing a routine for these reviews, whether weekly or monthly, helps keep your business on track. Additionally, consider involving your team in these goals and progress reviews.

When everyone understands the targets and their role in achieving them, it fosters a collective effort towards success.

The Impact on Your Business and Personal Goals

Achieving your business financial goals has a ripple effect on your personal financial aspirations.

As your business grows and becomes more profitable, you may find yourself able to invest more in personal pursuits, whether that's upgrading your home, funding your children's education, or planning for retirement.

It's essential to regularly revisit both your business and personal goals to ensure they remain aligned and mutually supportive.

The discipline and strategic thinking required to achieve business goals can translate to personal finance management.

The same principles of setting SMART goals, creating actionable plans, and maintaining accountability apply to personal finances.

For example, if part of your personal goal is to save for a dream vacation, you can use similar strategies: determine the total cost, set a savings target, and break it down into manageable monthly savings goals.

In summary, setting and achieving financial goals in your home improvement business not only propels your business forward but also enhances your personal financial well-being.

By systematically calculating your targets, developing strategic plans, and maintaining accountability, you create a solid foundation for both your business successes and personal financial security.

Calculating and Increasing Your Average Job Size

For any home improvement business, one of the key metrics to monitor is the Average Job Size (AJS).

This figure represents the average revenue generated per project and directly influences your overall profitability.

Calculating your AJS is straightforward: simply divide your total revenue by the number of jobs completed over a specific period. For instance, if you earned $100,000 from 50 projects in a year, your AJS would be $2,000.

Tips to Increase Your Average Job Size

1. **Upselling and Cross-Selling**: Identify additional services or products that complement the primary project. For example, if you're installing a new kitchen, offer upgrades like premium countertops, backsplashes, or advanced appliances. These add-ons not only enhance the client's experience but also increase your job size.

2. **Tiered Service Packages**:
Create tiered packages that offer varying levels of service. For instance, a basic package could cover essential services, while a premium package includes extras such as extended warranties, post-installation maintenance, or high-end materials. This gives clients options while encouraging them to opt for more comprehensive—and higher-priced—solutions.

3. **Client Education**:
Educate your clients on the value of quality and longevity. Often, clients may opt for cheaper solutions without understanding the long-term benefits of premium options. Providing informative materials, case studies, or even testimonials can help them see the value in investing more upfront.

4. **Bundling Services**:
Offer bundled services at a slight discount compared to purchasing each service individually. This can make clients feel they are getting more value for their money while increasing the overall job size. For example, bundle roofing with gutter installation and offer a slight discount to encourage clients to take on more services.

5. **Leverage Technology:**
   Use software to track and analyze data related to your projects. CRM systems can help identify trends and opportunities for upselling or cross-selling. Additionally, detailed project management software can ensure that projects are executed smoothly, enhancing customer satisfaction and encouraging repeat business.

Impact on Your Business and Goals

Increasing your Average Job Size can have a profound impact on your business. Higher job sizes mean more revenue per project, which can significantly boost your bottom line without the need to increase the number of projects you take on.

This allows for better resource allocation, improved cash flow, and the ability to invest in higher-quality materials and skilled labor, ultimately leading to higher client satisfaction and more referrals.

A higher AJS can help you achieve your business goals more quickly. Whether you're aiming to expand your operations, invest in new technology, or simply improve your profit margins, increasing your average job size can provide the financial flexibility to do so.

It also helps in building a more sustainable business model where you can focus on quality over quantity, leading to long-term success and stability.

In conclusion, focusing on increasing your Average Job Size is not just about boosting revenue; it's about creating value for your clients, enhancing your service offerings, and positioning your business for sustainable growth.

By implementing these strategies, you can ensure that each project contributes more significantly to your financial health and business objectives.

Understanding Long-Term Client Value

Long-term client value (LTCV) is a crucial metric for any home improvement business owner aiming to ensure sustainable growth.

LTCV refers to the total revenue a client generates over the course of their relationship with your business. By focusing on LTCV, you gain insights into the profitability of your client base and can strategize effectively to enhance it.

Calculating Long-Term Client Value

To calculate LTCV, you need to gather data on your clients' purchasing behavior. Start by identifying the average purchase value, the frequency of purchases, and the average client lifespan. The formula is straightforward:

LTCV = Average Purchase Value x Purchase Frequency x Customer Lifespan

For example, if a client typically spends $500 per project, hires you twice a year, and remains a client for 5 years, the LTCV would be:

LTCV = $500 x 2 x 5 = $5,000

This calculation helps you understand how much revenue a single client brings in, allowing you to allocate resources more effectively towards client retention and acquisition strategies that maximize this value.

Strategies to Increase Long-Term Client Value

1. **Build Strong Relationships:**
   Develop a rapport with your clients by maintaining regular communication and offering personalized services. A satisfied client is more likely to return for future projects and recommend your services to others.
2. **Offer Loyalty Programs:**
   Implement a loyalty program that rewards clients for repeated business. Discounts, exclusive offers, or even a simple points system can incentivize clients to continue choosing your services over competitors.
3. **Upsell and Cross-Sell:**
   Train your team to identify opportunities for upselling and cross-selling. Offering premium services or additional relevant products can increase the average purchase value per client.

4. **Solicit Feedback and Act on It:** Regularly seek client feedback and make improvements based on their suggestions. Demonstrating that you value their opinions will enhance client satisfaction and loyalty.
5. **Provide Exceptional Customer Service:** Ensure your customer service is top-notch. Prompt responses, problem resolution, and courteous interactions go a long way in retaining clients.

Impact on Your Business and Goals

Increasing LTCV has a profound impact on your business. Higher client value translates to increased revenue, allowing you to invest more in marketing, technology, and employee development.

It also stabilizes your cash flow, making financial planning more predictable and less risky. Ultimately, a higher LTCV fosters a strong, loyal client base, which is invaluable for long-term business sustainability and growth.

By focusing on calculating and increasing LTCV, you are not only improving your immediate revenue but also setting the foundation for a thriving home improvement business that can achieve its long-term goals.

Remember, happy and loyal clients are the bedrock of any successful business.

Knowing Your Value

It's vital to recognize and uphold your worth.

Often, the temptation to lower your standards, reduce your rates, or work with ill-fitting clients is strong.

However, undervaluing yourself not only detracts from your inherent value but also prevents you from delivering the top-tier service your clients expect.

It also undermines the credibility of both you and your brand, which you've worked tirelessly to establish.

Remember, compromising your value for quick financial gains is a short-sighted approach that can hinder your long-term success and sustainability.

An important lesson I learned early on is encapsulated in the phrase, "I would rather be known as the expensive guy than the cheap guy."

It took some time to fully grasp this concept, but its wisdom is profound.

People tend to associate and do business with individuals who reflect their own values and standards.

The saying, "You are the average of the top 5 people you hang around," holds true.

By consistently offering your services at a discounted rate, you inadvertently attract clients who are looking for cheap work.

This creates a cycle where every referral expects the same low prices, diminishing your value.

Conversely, by charging what you're worth, clients will recognize the quality and justify the cost, leading to referrals that appreciate and are willing to pay for premium service.

My journey taught me the hard way that accepting underpriced projects just to secure work is not a sustainable strategy.

Initially, I succumbed to clients' demands to lower my prices, which led to a chain of undervalued referrals and a lot of work for little reward.

This not only stunted my financial growth but also restricted my ability to invest in and improve my business.

The turning point came when I decided to raise my prices to reflect the quality of service I provide.

Although it was challenging and resulted in losing some clients, it was a necessary step towards growth.

By charging what I was worth, I attracted clients who valued my work, allowing me to enhance their experience and build a stronger brand.

Knowing your value and not being afraid to charge accordingly is crucial for long-term success.

It ensures that you can provide exceptional service, grow your business, and achieve your goals without compromising your worth.

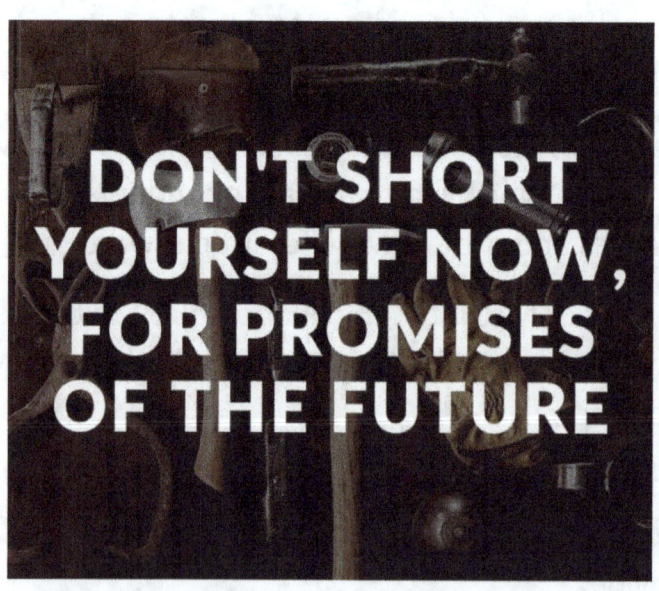

Chapter SEVRN: Pillar 5: Your Team - The Builders of Your Vision

A well-constructed team is the pillar upon which all operational efficiency, customer satisfaction, and ultimately, business growth is built.

This chapter dives into why prioritizing team development is crucial in your contracting business and how it can be the difference between merely surviving and thriving in the industry.

Building a strong team goes beyond hiring individuals with the right skills. It involves fostering a culture of collaboration, respect, and continuous learning.

In the contracting business, where projects are often complex and deadlines tight, a cohesive team can efficiently navigate challenges, innovate solutions, and maintain high standards of workmanship.

This synergy not only enhances productivity but also elevates the morale of the team, leading to improved job satisfaction and lower turnover rates.

Remember, a team that works well together is more resilient in the face of adversity and more adaptable to change, two inevitable aspects of the contracting business.

A strong team is your business's best ambassador. Clients interact with your employees at every stage of a project, from initial consultations to final execution.

How your team handles these interactions can significantly impact your business's reputation.

A team that communicates effectively, exhibits professionalism, and shows genuine commitment to meeting clients' needs can elevate your business's standing in the marketplace, leading to repeat business and valuable referrals.

Investing in your team's development, therefore, is not just about improving operational efficiency; it's about building a brand that is synonymous with quality, reliability, and exceptional service.

While the temptation might be to focus on the technical aspects of your contracting business, it's essential to remember that your team is the most valuable asset you have.

By investing in creating a supportive, skilled, and motivated team, you lay down a robust foundation for your business to grow.

This investment will pay dividends in the form of higher productivity, better customer relations, and ultimately, a stronger, more resilient business that is well-positioned for long-term success in the competitive contracting industry.

Administration: The Backbone of Your Business

The administrative team serves as the backbone of your business, playing an indispensable role in ensuring smooth and efficient operations behind the scenes.

This dedicated team is responsible for a wide array of crucial tasks, ranging from financial management and scheduling to compliance and customer service.

Their expertise and meticulous attention to detail allow other departments to concentrate on their core responsibilities without being overwhelmed by the complexities of daily operations.

By efficiently managing finances, the administrative team ensures that budgets are adhered to, invoices are processed promptly, and financial reports are accurate.

This financial stability is essential for making informed business decisions and maintaining the company's overall health.

In terms of scheduling, they coordinate various projects and appointments, ensuring that timelines are met and resources are optimally utilized.

Compliance is another critical area, where the administrative team ensures that the business adheres to industry regulations and standards, thereby avoiding legal pitfalls and maintaining a good standing in the industry.

Their role in customer service cannot be overstated. By handling inquiries, resolving issues, and maintaining open lines of communication, the administrative team fosters strong relationships with clients, which is vital for repeat business and positive referrals.

Your administrative team provides a stable and reliable platform upon which all other business activities can flourish.

Their unwavering support and behind-the-scenes diligence enable the company to scale new heights, driving growth and ensuring long-term success.

Production: The Heart of Quality and Efficiency

At the core of any successful business lies its production team, the driving force where your services truly come to life.

This dedicated group of professionals is responsible for the meticulous execution of projects, transforming ideas and plans into reality.

The hallmarks of a robust production team include exceptional workmanship, efficiency in operations, strict adherence to timelines, and unwavering commitment to safety protocols.

These attributes not only contribute to the seamless completion of projects but also enhance the overall quality and reliability of your business offerings.

The expertise and diligence of your production team are pivotal in ensuring the success of every project undertaken.

Their ability to deliver high-quality results consistently not only satisfies customers but also significantly boosts your business's reputation.

A strong reputation built on excellence and reliability attracts new clients and retains existing ones, fostering a cycle of trust and loyalty.

When customers are pleased with the outcomes, they are more likely to return for future services and recommend your business to others. This word-of-mouth promotion is invaluable, driving organic growth and expanding your customer base.

A well-functioning production team contributes to the overall efficiency of your business operations. By streamlining processes and minimizing waste, they help in reducing costs and maximizing productivity.

This efficiency translates into better profitability and a competitive edge in the market.

Investing in a capable and motivated production team is an investment in the future success and sustainability of your business.

Their role is not just about completing tasks; it's about building a foundation of quality and efficiency that propels your business forward.

Sales and Marketing: The Growth Drivers

Sales and marketing teams, though distinct in their functions, are integral to propelling a business toward sustained growth.

These teams share the ultimate objective of attracting new customers while retaining existing ones, but they achieve this through different yet complementary approaches.

The sales team is primarily responsible for converting leads into clients. This involves personalized outreach, relationship-building, and understanding the specific needs and pain points of potential customers to offer tailored solutions that meet their requirements.

Through persistent efforts and a focus on customer satisfaction, the sales team ensures that prospects transition smoothly into loyal clients.

The marketing team is tasked with creating visibility for the business and establishing a strong brand presence in the market.

Their strategies encompass a wide range of activities, including digital marketing, content creation, social media engagements, advertising campaigns, and organizing events.

By leveraging these diverse channels, the marketing team generates valuable leads and drives awareness about the business's offerings.

They work to position the company as a thought leader and a trusted provider in its industry, thereby attracting a broader audience and nurturing potential clients until they are ready to engage with the sales team.

Together, the synergy between sales and marketing creates a powerful engine that fuels business growth. Marketing generates a steady stream of qualified leads and enhances the company's reputation, while sales converts these leads into clients through targeted, personalized efforts.

This seamless collaboration ensures that the business not only attracts new projects but also fosters long-term relationships with clients, driving sustained growth and success.

Effective communication and alignment between these teams are crucial, as they collectively contribute to the overarching goal of business expansion and profitability.

Relationship Partners: Expanding Your Business Reach

Growing a profitable home improvement business hinges significantly on the strength and quality of your relationships with key partners, including vendors, subcontractors, and industry peers. These relationships are foundational to your business's ability to expand and maintain sustainability.

Partnering with reliable vendors and suppliers can lead to advantageous cost savings and ensure access to the latest materials and technologies, keeping your business at the forefront of innovation.

Subcontractors, on the other hand, provide the expertise and manpower necessary to handle more extensive and diverse projects, allowing your business to offer a broader range of services to clients.

Industry peers can offer valuable insights, share best practices, and even collaborate on large-scale projects, facilitating entry into new markets and elevating your business's reputation.

Cultivating these partnerships requires consistent effort and strategic nurturing. Building trust and maintaining open communication with your suppliers can lead to favorable terms and priority access to new products.

Establishing clear agreements and fostering a culture of respect and reliability with subcontractors ensures that projects run smoothly and meet high standards.

Engaging with industry peers through networking events, industry conferences, and professional associations can open doors to collaborative opportunities and knowledge-sharing that benefit all parties involved.

By investing in these relationships, you create a robust network of allies that support your business's growth through collaboration and mutual benefits.

Building a Life and Business with Family at the Core

Chris Wysokowski Painting was born out of necessity and a deep-seated desire to provide a better life for my family.

In 2005, the birth of my first daughter ignited a fire within me that I had never known before. I wanted to offer her the stability and opportunities that my own childhood had lacked.

By 2009, I took the plunge and started my own painting business. Shortly after, in 2010, I married my wonderful wife, and we welcomed our second daughter into the world.

With a growing family, the pressure to succeed intensified. I was determined to be the provider they deserved, but the journey was far from easy.

At first, I believed that hard work alone would guarantee success. I was always on time, never shied away from long hours, and rarely missed a day of work unless I was ill.

However, despite my diligent efforts, we often struggled to make ends meet. The long hours took a toll on my family life, and I missed countless precious moments with my wife and children.

It took me years to understand that running a successful business required more than just a strong work ethic.

It required knowledge, strategy, and the right support system—things I hadn't learned from anyone.

The turning point came around 2018 when I finally realized the importance of setting goals, developing systems, and investing in personal growth.

I sought out mentors, industry events, and reading books. These changes didn't just transform my business; they transformed my life.

By the time my son was born in 2020, amidst the challenges of the COVID-19 pandemic, I had a clear mission: to help others build, grow, and maximize their own businesses and lives.

This mission led to the creation of Service Industry Empire, where I now dedicate myself to guiding other home improvement business owners toward success.

Today, my family and I enjoy a level of stability and happiness that once seemed out of reach.

We have our own home, and I cherish the time I can now spend with my wife and children.

Together, we are working toward future goals, driven by the lessons learned from our struggles.

By focusing on what truly matters—family, personal growth, and effective systems—I've been able to build a thriving business and a fulfilling life.

When it comes to my team, when I first embarked on the journey of starting my own home improvement business, I was filled with a mixture of excitement and trepidation.

My brothers, always my greatest supporters, agreed to help me paint and tackle various projects, even though they were all novices in the field.

What we lacked in experience, we made up for in determination and a strong work ethic.

However, the initial days were riddled with challenges, not the least of which was my lack of systems and knowledge about successfully running a business.

My brothers often didn't get paid on time, and when they did, it wasn't nearly what they deserved. This strained our relationships, yet their unwavering support never wavered.

As time went on, I slowly but surely, I began to implement better systems for project management, client relations, and financial oversight.

The improvements were not immediate, but gradually, we started to see positive changes.

Our projects were completed more efficiently, clients were happier, and I was finally able to pay my brothers what they deserved as well as what I deserved.

Although not all of my brothers work with me now, I am forever grateful for the unwavering support of my brothers, which made this success possible.

Looking back, I am proud of the progress we've made and the obstacles we've overcome.

The journey from a small, struggling startup to a thriving, respected business has been nothing short of remarkable.

Each project we complete successfully is a testament to our collective effort and the lessons we've learned along the way.

In reflecting on this journey, I am reminded of the importance of never giving up, even when the odds seem insurmountable.

The support of my family, the willingness to continuously learn and adapt, and the sheer determination to succeed have been the foundation of our growth.

As we move forward, I am excited about the future possibilities and committed to upholding the values that got us here.

Here's to many more years of building not just homes, but also dreams and lasting relationships.

Chapter EIGHT: Bring It All Together With Consistency

In the world of home improvement contracting, where myriad factors such as economic fluctuations, client preferences, and technological advancements can sway your business trajectory, one principle stands as the unwavering foundation of unstoppable growth: consistency.

This section explores the multifaceted role of consistency in building a robust, thriving home improvement business, highlighting strategies for embedding this critical principle into your operational, marketing, and customer service frameworks.

At the heart of every successful home improvement business lies a commitment to consistent quality.

Quality should not be a variable, fluctuating with the size of the project or the client's prominence, but a constant that distinguishes your services in a competitive market.

This steadfast dedication to excellence across all projects not only cultivates a strong brand reputation but also fosters client trust and loyalty.

Implementing rigorous quality control processes and continuous staff training ensures that your team not only meets but exceeds client expectations, project after project.

For instance, adopting standardized procedures for inspections and utilizing checklists can help maintain a uniform standard of excellence, ensuring that every job, whether big or small, receives the same level of meticulous attention.

However, consistency extends far beyond the quality of workmanship; it encompasses every facet of your business operations.

In marketing, a consistent message and branding across all platforms reinforce your company's identity and values, resonating with your target audience and building a cohesive brand image.

Whether it's through your website, social media, or traditional advertising, maintaining a uniform tone and style helps potential clients recognize and remember your brand, making them more likely to choose your services when the need arises.

For example, using a consistent color scheme, logo, and tagline across all marketing materials can create a memorable brand presence that stands out in a crowded marketplace.

Regular engagement through newsletters or blog posts can keep your brand top-of-mind for prospective clients.

Customer service, a critical component of any service-oriented business, thrives on consistency.

Clients expect reliable, courteous, and efficient interactions at every touchpoint, from the initial inquiry to the final project walkthrough.

Consistent, positive customer experiences build trust and can turn one-time clients into lifelong advocates for your business.

By implementing standardized customer service protocols and training your team in effective communication and problem-solving techniques, you ensure that every client receives the same high level of service, regardless of the project size or complexity.

For example, developing a script for handling common client inquiries and concerns can ensure that your team provides clear and helpful information consistently, while regular feedback sessions can help identify areas for improvement in your service delivery.

Consistency is not merely a goal but a guiding principle that permeates every aspect of a successful business.

It builds a foundation of trust with clients, establishes a strong brand identity, and ensures that your business can withstand the challenges of an ever-evolving market.

By prioritizing consistency in quality, marketing, and customer service, you set your business on a path to long-term success and sustainability.

As you move forward, embed consistency into the DNA of your business, ensuring that it not only survives but thrives.

Whether through the adoption of advanced project management software to streamline operations or the establishment of a comprehensive customer relationship management system, these tools and strategies will empower you to maintain high standards that set your business apart.

Chapter NINE: The Power of Action and Implementation

Now, it's time to discuss the critical importance of taking action and implementing these concepts to transform your business and achieve your goals.

Understanding the theories and strategies behind each pillar is crucial, but the real magic happens when you put these ideas into practice.

Imagine running a painting business where every stroke of the brush not only beautifies a home but also contributes to your company's growth and profitability.

This vision is entirely achievable, but it requires action. Action transforms theoretical knowledge into tangible results, enabling you to see real improvements in your business operations and financial outcomes.

By actively working on your mindset, you'll cultivate the resilience and adaptability needed to face challenges head-on.

Implementing effective marketing systems will increase your visibility and attract more clients.

A streamlined sales process ensures that those leads are converted into profitable projects. Monitoring your financial health allows you to make informed decisions that optimize profitability.

Finally, investing in your team ensures that everyone is aligned with your business goals, driving productivity and innovation.

Bridging the Gap: From Goals to Reality

Every business owner sets goals, but the journey from setting those goals to achieving them can be daunting.

This book provides you with the roadmap, but you must take the steps.

Start by setting clear, actionable objectives for each pillar.

For instance, if your goal is to improve your marketing system, begin by identifying your target audience and creating a compelling brand message.

Implement digital marketing techniques such as social media campaigns or search engine optimization to increase your online presence.

In the sales domain, develop a script or process that your team can follow to ensure consistency and effectiveness.

Train your team to understand client needs and communicate value effectively.

Financially, set up regular reviews of your costs, margins, and cash flow to stay on top of your financial health.

For your team, create development plans, foster a positive culture, and recognize their contributions to keep them motivated and aligned with your vision.

The Ripple Effect of Implementation

Taking action and implementing the strategies outlined in this book will have a profound impact on your business.

As you start to see the results of your efforts, you'll build momentum, which will drive further improvements.

Each successful implementation reinforces the foundation of your business, making it more resilient and better equipped to handle market fluctuations and competition.

The benefits will extend beyond your business.

Achieving your business goals leads to personal satisfaction and financial security. It provides the freedom to pursue other passions and spend more time with loved ones.

By building a profitable and sustainable business, you contribute to the economy, create jobs, and enhance the living spaces of your clients.

The journey to building your business is paved with action and implementation.

The five pillars provide the foundation, but it's your commitment to taking action that will turn your entrepreneurial dreams into reality.

Embrace the strategies outlined in this book, implement them with dedication, and watch as your business reaches new heights of success.

The power to transform your business and achieve your goals is in your hands—take action today.

In Conclusion…

As we draw the curtain on "Foundation First: The 5 Pillars of Unstoppable growth in Your Home Improvement Business," it's clear that we've embarked on a journey of transformation and empowerment.

This book has not just provided a blueprint for building a unstoppable contracting business; it has ignited a flame of ambition and determination to achieve excellence in an industry that demands nothing less.

The journey from the first page to the last is a testament to the power of foundational principles in creating a business that not only survives but thrives in the competitive landscape of contracting.

The benefits and results that await those who take action after reading this book are limitless.

Imagine a business where financial health is not just a goal but a reality, where your brand stands out as a beacon of excellence in a sea of competition, where every lead is a step towards a loyal customer, and where your team is not just employees but partners in success.

"Foundation First" has laid out the path to achieving these outcomes, emphasizing that the journey requires commitment, resilience, and an unwavering belief in the principles that underpin lasting success.

Embrace the lessons of "Foundation First" and step into a future where your contracting business is not just a player in the industry but a leader.

This book has equipped you with the knowledge, strategies, and mindset to elevate your business.

The journey ahead is yours to shape, fueled by the foundational pillars of success. Let "Foundation First" be your guide, your inspiration, and your blueprint to building a legacy in the contracting industry that is marked by prosperity, achievement, and fulfillment.

The path to unparalleled success begins with a foundation first, and the time to start building is now.

The "You Win First" Guarantee

At The Unlimited Contractor, our mission is to serve you at the highest level by empowering home improvement business owners to achieve remarkable growth and transform their enterprises. We recognize that investing in coaching is a significant commitment, which is why we have created the "You Win First" Guarantee to provide you with peace of mind and ensure your success.

What is the "You Win First" Guarantee?

Our "You Win First" Guarantee reflects our unwavering commitment to your success. We are so confident in the value and effectiveness of our coaching that we are willing to take the risk upfront. Here's what it includes:

Risk-Free Coaching Experience:

- **One Month of Free Coaching**: Experience one full month of personalized coaching at no cost. This opportunity allows you to witness the transformative impact of our strategies on your business growth firsthand.
- **Tailored Strategies**: Throughout this month, we will collaborate closely with you to identify your unique challenges and goals, crafting customized strategies that align with your specific business needs.
- **Dedicated Support**: Our team of experienced coaches will provide ongoing support, guidance, and resources to ensure you implement effective practices that lead to measurable results.

Results-Oriented Approach:

- **Focus on Growth**: Our primary goal is to help you expand your home improvement business. We monitor key performance indicators and milestones to assess your progress and ensure you're on the path to success.
- **No Payment Until You See Results**: We are confident in our coaching program's ability to deliver results, which is why we don't require any payment until you are satisfied with the progress and tangible outcomes achieved during the first month.

How It Works:

1. **Initial Consultation**: Start with a free consultation to discuss your business objectives and challenges.
2. **Customized Coaching Plan**: We develop a tailored coaching plan designed to address your specific needs and accelerate growth.
3. **One Month of Coaching**: Engage in a month of comprehensive coaching sessions, implementing strategies, and receiving continuous support.
4. **Evaluation and Decision**: At the end of the month, you'll evaluate the growth and improvements in your business. Only if you are satisfied with the results will you choose to continue with our coaching services and proceed with payment.

Why Choose Us?

- **Expertise in Home Improvement Business**: Our coaches specialize in the home improvement sector, bringing valuable industry-specific knowledge and insights.
- **Proven Track Record**: We have a history of helping businesses like yours achieve significant growth and financial success.
- **Commitment to Your Success**: Your success is our priority. We are dedicated to ensuring you see positive changes before any financial commitment is required.

With the "You Win First" Guarantee, you have nothing to lose and everything to gain.

Begin your journey towards a more prosperous home improvement business today with confidence and assurance.

Contact us now to start your risk-free coaching adventure!

Scan Me

Start Winning Now

Today is MINE "OWN IT"

One Day at a Time

WHAT ARE MY GOALS FOR TODAY?

- _____
- _____
- _____
- _____

WHAT AM I GRATEFUL FOR TODAY?

- _____
- _____
- _____
- _____

WHAT CAN I COMMIT TO DOING TODAY TO REACH MY GOALS?

- _____
- _____
- _____
- _____

PROGRESS OVER PERFECTION

FOCUS ON THE SOLUTIONS, NOT THE PROBLEMS

POSITIVE THOUGHTS LEAD TO POSITIVE ACTIONS

TAKE CONTROL OF YOUR EMPIRE

CONQUER THE MOMEMT

FAITH OVER FEAR

WHO CAN I HELP TODAY?

- _____
- _____

WHO CAN I TALK TO TODAY?

- _____
- _____

Mindset Matters

CIRCLE HOW YOU FEEL

START OF DAY   END OF DAY

😊 😐 ☹️   😊 😐 ☹️

HOW I RATE MY PROGRESS TODAY

1 2 3 4 5 6 7 8 9 10

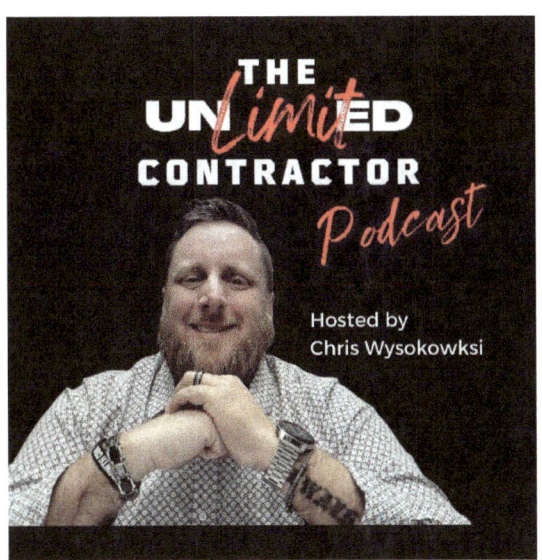

Join us on this transformative journey with "The Unlimited Contractor" and embark on the path to converting your Home Improvement Business into an EMPIRE of success. With each episode, you'll gain invaluable insights and tools to help you build, grow, and sustain a thriving business empire.

Scan Me

The Ultimate Contractor Toolkit

"Unlock Your Business's Potential: The Ultimate Toolkit for Scaling Success!"

- ✓ More Free Time
- ✓ Higher Profits
- ✓ Generate More Leads
- ✓ Create A Business You Love

Scan Me

For taking the first steps towards building your empire we want to give you this toolkit as a bonus

Scan Me

Use code SIE60 to
get a 60 day free trial
This is a paid affiliate link

The easiest way to get 4x more reviews and up to 2x more customers

Find the perfect solution for your local business.

★★★★★ 4.9 Trusted by thousands of companies

Scan Me

Get your 14 day free trial

This is a paid affiliate link

Empower Your KINGDOMS And You Will Create An EMPIRE

www.ingramcontent.com/pod-product-compliance
Lightning Source LLC
Chambersburg PA
CBHW052255220526
45471CB00001B/342